A
BRUSH
WITH
ANGELS

A BRUSH WITH ANGELS

Compelling Tales of Biblical Proportion

By Gary Myers

LEAFWOOD
PUBLISHERS

A BRUSH WITH ANGELS

Compelling Tales of Biblical Proportion

Copyright 2011 by Gary Myers

ISBN 978-0-89112-290-6
LCCN 2011017960

Printed in the United States of America

LIBRARY OF CONGRESS CATALOGING-IN-PUBLICATION DATA
Myers, G. A., 1955-
A brush with angels : compelling tales of biblical proportion / by Gary Myers.
    p. cm.
Includes bibliographical references and index.
ISBN 978-0-89112-290-6 (alk. paper)
1. Angels--Biblical teaching. 2. Bible stories, English. I. Title.
BS680.A48M948 2011
235'.3--dc23
                                                                    2011017960

Cover design by Thinkpen Design, LLC
Interior text design by Sandy Armstrong

Leafwood Publishers is an imprint of
Abilene Christian University Press
1626 Campus Court
Abilene, Texas 79601

1-877-816-4455
www.leafwoodpublishers.com

11 12 13 14 15 16 / 7 6 5 4 3 2 1

Dedication

I dedicate this book to my children, Gabriel, Hannah, Samara, and Elyssa. I don't know any child, or children, who know their father as well as you. In some ways that is quite wonderful and in other ways it can be quite miserable. You have seen me at my best and my worst, and loved me through every scenario. You have loved me and given me courage when I could find none on my own. When my professional world seemed to be toppling you reminded me that God had never failed me and he would not do so then. You were right, of course. When I felt very alone, you were the arms that wrapped around me and made me understand love that never fails.

As you face this life I pray that it will be with fearless and faithful hearts. I pray that somewhere and sometime you feel the brush of an angel's wing and know that God has his messengers eagerly running to your aid. They will come when you least expect it and God will do his work at just the right time. May prayer pour lavishly from your lips, may your arms often be lifted in worship, and may you always be certain that heaven knows your name.

CONTENTS

SECTION FIVE: RECEIVE

SECTION SIX: GIVE

PREFACE

A Brush with Angels was written to inspire and ignite a renewed passion for the truth of God's real presence and love in your heart. We live in a world that can make us wonder if anyone really cares about what happens to us on any level. Daily life can turn faith and compassion brittle and apathetic. I have seen it happen many times on both a personal and professional level.

All my life I have been a student of Scripture and fascinated with storytelling. Whether in my worship leading, teaching, writing, or work as a publisher, I have always gone out of my way to use stories to instruct, inspire, and encourage. That is where this book comes from—love for the Word and a passion for stories. As I have poured over the adventures of King David, the life of Christ, and the Acts of the Apostles, I have pictured the events in full color . . . always taking the story even further. When I read the story of the woman healed of bleeding, I expanded the story imagining in my mind what the woman's life was like, what she looked like, what her parents were like, and so on. Every time I read stories like this one I feel closer to the woman and her plight, and more able to picture myself there in the crowd that witnessed the event. That is what led to the pages you are about to read.

As you read this book I want you to feel as though you are in the crowd watching the woman touch the cloak of Jesus, to feel the heat of the day, and experience the pushing of the crowd and the exhilaration of a woman set free from a life-long illness. I want you to walk into the home of Mary as she is visited by an angel with staggering news; I want you to feel the brush of the angel's wing. That is what these stories are. They are biblical stories you have read before—but not like this. As you read, you will see that I have left each scriptural account intact in the story but have filled in around it with fictional portraits of those involved. At the end of each chapter you will be able to read the entire passage as it is found in God's Word.

In some cases I have written the stories from multiple perspectives. For example, in the story of the angel visiting Mary, you will read from the angel's view as well as from Mary's. These writings have changed how I read many familiar passages. I humbly hope they will do the same for you, making them more alive than ever.

Most of all, I hope that this book brings you closer to the one who broke through our human experience in order to relate to us in every way possible. Perhaps when you read you may find yourself touching the cloak of Jesus or hearing his voice tell you not to cry. Maybe you will find yourself right there in the story when the angel tells the disciples to remember that Jesus is coming back just as he went—I hope for this with all my heart. It has been both a heart rending and wonderful journey for me to enter these stories upon a fresh and powerful path. May you feel the same as you read.

Section One

CHOSEN

1

CHOSEN BY HEAVEN

Introduction

The Word can bring either feelings of exhilaration or defeat, anticipation or fear. Those fortunate enough to have been gifted with dazzling beauty, amazing athletic ability, or tremendous talent frequently know the excitement of being chosen. They're chosen as special dates, as participants of winning teams, or as main characters in plays. Others, not so blessed in these physical ways know well the deflating feeling of rejection when they're cut from a team or when they sit by a phone that just doesn't ring. You yourself may have felt the sting of tears after hearing that you weren't quite up to fulfilling that vital purpose or starring in the role you hungered to play. You also may know the sense of pride and fulfillment that comes from being a chosen one.

No matter who we are, we ache to be chosen, because being chosen somehow validates our existence. It means we matter, that we're noticed and appreciated. Above all, it means that someone believes in us.

Hear God's message of good news: someone does believe in you. And that someone has chosen you—not because of your beauty or talent but because of his limitless love. This is no ordinary someone; this is the Lord of lords, the King of kings. He has spent the last two thousand years with your name on his lips and in his heart. He has reached across time to place his nail-scarred hand on your shoulder and say, "I have chosen you."

And now, you are his. You have been chosen to accomplish something very special, something with eternal implications, something that matches the gifts he has given you. Perhaps you've been chosen to parent a child who will ultimately bring peace to our world. Or maybe your task is simply to dry the eyes and heal the hurting heart of a friend. It could be that you've been chosen to share a meal with a hungry person who has a thirsty soul, to be a deeply devoted spouse in a world without loyalties, or to encourage fellow employees when naked cynicism is the standard expression. When circumstances in your life make you feel unwanted or unimportant, just remember—you are chosen. Chosen by love and gifted by grace, you will soon see the One who chose you face to face.

Chosen by Heaven

He had been on alert for days. He was becoming restless, wondering not only when he would be called into action, but what his crucially important mission would entail. The archangel Gabriel had experienced every major battle between heaven and earth since the beginning of time. He had witnessed the disheartening and devastating fall of his previous leader, Lucifer, and the archangels who had decided to follow, many of whom had served the Father alongside Gabriel. He knew only that the message he would soon carry to earth would put into motion the event on which all history would hinge. The weight of its importance impassioned him as nothing had before. Questions ran through his mind: *Where on earth will I be sent with my message? Whom has the Father chosen to receive it? Will I face fierce opposition as I did on my way to minister to Daniel, or is Lucifer still blindly looking for the key to the Father's plan?*

Finally, the orders arrived. They came from the Father and were delivered by Michael, who smiled with excitement as he told Gabriel of his destination: "You are to deliver a message of good news from the Father. Go to Nazareth, a town in Galilee, to a virgin pledged to be married to a man named Joseph, a descendant of David. The virgin's name is

Mary. You may face opposition, so be prepared. This is the time we have all been waiting for, my friend." Several angels who had accompanied Michael embraced Gabriel, one by one. As they shared in the excitement and anticipation, they said to one another, "May the Father's will be done."

On his way to Nazareth, Gabriel found himself wondering what kind of woman this Mary would be. As he walked the streets of Nazareth's poorest districts, he couldn't help feeling surprised: from this small, unimpressive town would come the hope for humankind. It made him all the more eager to meet the woman the Father had chosen to bring the Messiah into the world. As he neared her home, his excitement grew.

Invisibly, Gabriel slipped into Mary's home and found the chosen one in her room. Gabriel had to smile as he watched her move energetically across the room and say to herself, "Soon I will be wed to the most wonderful man in all of Israel. God has been so good to me." Because of the enormity of the responsibility God was about to place on this woman, Gabriel had thought Mary would be much older. But she was a young girl.

Gabriel's curiosity grew. What was it about this young girl that made her so special? Of all the women on earth, why had God chosen her? As Gabriel was puzzling over his questions, Mary knelt on the floor. Curious as to what she would do next, Gabriel moved in closer. Mary bowed her head reverently, clasped her hands before her chest, and began to pray.

"Almighty God, I seek you with all my heart. In my poverty you have made me rich; in my times of fear you have given me courage; in my pain you have soothed my heart; in my youth you have made me content." Intensely moved by the depth of her prayer, Gabriel placed his hand gently on her shoulder. To his surprise, Mary turned her cheek as if to nuzzle his hand. She concluded her prayer, "I ask nothing more than to serve you all the days of my life, for my life is worth nothing if not lived to your glory."

Gabriel was stunned. He had not heard such heartfelt words for at least three generations. The prayers of most had become nothing more than rote phrases and trite requests.

Still unseen, Gabriel moved closer to her and searched her face. Her dark eyes were full of excitement. Her olive skin was unblemished and soft. Her black hair, though covered, was thick and long. But most of all he saw that this girl possessed a holy heart, one of immense devotion, a heart that could be trusted with the news he was about to reveal.

Gabriel knew enough of the Father's plan to realize that this innocent, spiritually-minded girl was about to hear the most wonderful news history would ever record. He also knew that in time she would be wounded by the deepest pain a mother could experience. Gabriel felt his face tighten and his arms flex. In a voice she could not hear, Gabriel whispered, "Your unspeakable joy will be matched by unimaginable sorrow. May God bless you, my child. It is easy to understand why the Father has chosen you."

Gabriel arose and made himself visible. Shocked, Mary stood and stepped away from Gabriel as he said, "Greetings, you who are highly favored! The Lord is with you." He wanted to cradle and soothe the startled girl as he shared his news, but he knew any such movement on his part would frighten her even more. "Do not be afraid, Mary," Gabriel said, "You have found favor with God. You will be with child and give birth to a son, and you are to give him the name Jesus. He will be great and will be called the Son of the Most High. The Lord God will give him the throne of his father David, and he will reign over the house of Jacob forever; his kingdom will never end."

As the news settled into Mary's heart, her expression turned to one of puzzlement, and she asked, "How will this be since I am a virgin?"

Gabriel moved closer, and she felt his warm touch on her shoulder. "The Holy Spirit will come upon you, and the power of the Most High will overshadow you. So the holy one to be born will be called the Son of God. Even Elizabeth your relative is going to have a child in her old age, and she, who was said to be barren, is in her sixth month." Then Gabriel, inspired by the magnitude of the unfolding events, proclaimed what every angel knows and Mary would soon learn: "For nothing is impossible with God."

Regaining her composure, Mary lifted her head and looked into Gabriel's kind eyes and said, "I am the Lord's servant. May it be to me as you have said." With that, Gabriel left her, rejoicing as he made his way to his heavenly dwelling.

Gabriel knew he would never forget his visit with the virgin through whom God would visit the world.

2

GOOD NEWS AND
A TRUSTED WOMAN

Introduction

It may have happened two thousand years ago, but within its storylines lives the most encouraging and inspiring message of all time. If you allow the hustle of life to push you through time panting and breathless, you will most certainly miss it. But don't. The message of the most beautiful story ever told has little to do with what you possess or accomplish and everything to do with who you are in the eyes of God. It can be summed up in one simple but wonderfully true statement: *God entrusts extraordinary things to very ordinary people.*

You see this truth in the lives of the participants in the message of God's Son coming to earth in the form of a baby—Mary the poor virgin, Joseph the blue-collar carpenter, and shepherds babysitting smelly sheep in a field.

If you were to describe the scene of Christ coming into the world as a portrait, you would have to say that the characters in the story were like rough, frayed burlap on which the golden brush of God painted the most precious moment in history. If you and I had painted the portrait, however, we would certainly have painted it on the finest canvas, and our characters would have been more worthy types—kings, wealthy aristocrats, responsible citizens, esteemed leaders. But we didn't paint it; God did.

And if you look into the beauty of God's portrait, you will plainly see a reflection. That's right, a reflection of your face, your weaknesses, your struggles, your future, and your ordinariness. Why? Because that's the kind of person to whom God entrusts his precious plans and purposes.

Do you feel you are just an ordinary person with an average life in a commonplace world? Good. You're just what God is looking for. You may be called upon to care for a special child, lend a hand and a heart to a hurting soul, or lift the spirits of a lonely life. Just don't let the glory of the Story pass you by. Stop, look, and listen. He trusts you to fulfill his mission.

Someday, someone may describe you as a burlap background on which God used his golden brush to paint a precious moment in history. In fact, the painting may already be under way.

Good News and a Trusted Woman

She took her position on the roof of the house and began the nightly ritual of brushing through her long, onyx hair. As the sun's orange blaze melted into the soft shades of dusk, Mary raised her nose and sniffed the evening air. She loved this time of year when the surrounding hills of Nazareth were filled with flowers. Every evening the sweet fragrances would ride the gentle wind into town and chase away the stale odors of animals and swirling dust. The youthful Mary took her perch here every day at the same time, after the evening meal was ended and everything was dutifully put away. She watched the neighborhood children play, and she laughed at their antics. She noticed other things as well.

She watched the men who gathered on the street to talk politics and business and to argue about Scripture. She knew their routine: they would begin their conversation calmly, but after a few minutes an argument would ensue. It always began with Perez, a long-bearded elderly man who lived a few houses away. In a hopeless sort of whine, he would complain about how the government was ruining Israel. Several others would join in with a hearty, "Amen!" Then Joseph, her Joseph, the man she would soon wed—the man with bright, bold eyes; strong energetic hands; and a deep, commanding voice—would always stand up on the side of faith and in defense of the promises of God.

That was what she had first noticed and loved about her Joseph—his faith, his strong, confident faith. Faith was in short supply in Israel at present, and she loved listening to him proclaim to the group that the Messiah was coming and coming very soon. The others would mumble under their breath about the hundreds of years since God had spoken in Israel. Did God still care about his people? Did he hear their cries? Joseph regularly concluded his discourse with, "Go ahead and hide behind your doubt if you wish; the God of my forefathers is faithful, and he will do what he has promised."

His words blew over Mary like a strong, refreshing wind. She whirled around and fell to her knees. With her arms uplifted and her long hair catching the south wind, she prayed, "God, thank you for hearing me; thank you for blessing my life with the words of the man with whom I will soon be one. I do believe you hear me when I pray. Send the Messiah to us, oh God. Send him on the faithful prayers of your servants who have not surrendered their faith. We wait for our deliverer, strong and mighty." With her eyes moist with tears of joy and hope, she rose and lifted her head to the now visible stars. She spoke her last five words forcefully and repeated them three times, "We trust you, oh God." Little did she know that as the heavens listened, a still, small voice answered, "And I trust you my child."

She suddenly felt the strong desire to be secluded—so alone that she would feel only the closeness of the God she loved and believed in. She moved from the roof to her small room and fell to her knees once more and raised her voice in joyous praise. Although she thought she was by herself, she was not. Although she believed her prayers were being heard by God alone, they were not. When she opened her eyes, she saw a bright glow emanating from behind her. She stood, turned, and stepped back in shock as the angelic being before her appeared in what seemed the radiance of a million candles.

"Greetings, you who are highly favored! The Lord is with you," Gabriel said. "Do not be afraid, Mary. You have found favor with God." She began to feel the warmth of an invisible embrace. Assurance quickly replaced her fear as she listened intently. "You will be with child and give birth to a son, and you are to give him the name Jesus. He will be great and will be called the Son of the Most High. The Lord God will give him the throne of his father David, and he will reign over the house of Jacob forever; his kingdom will never end."

As the news settled into Mary's heart, her expression changed from astonishment to bewilderment, and she asked, "How will this be since I am a virgin?"

Gabriel moved closer and reached out to touch her shoulder softly. As he felt her nervousness subside, he smiled and said, "The Holy Spirit will come upon you, and the power of the Most High will overshadow you. So the holy one to be born will be called the Son of God."

Mary almost felt herself say, "The Messiah . . . are you talking about the Messiah . . . coming through me?"

Sensing her doubt, Gabriel affirmed, "Even Elizabeth your relative is going to have a child in her old age, and she, who was said to be barren, is in her sixth month. For nothing is impossible with God."

As Mary lifted her head, the words echoed in her heart until she fully believed them. She looked deeply into Gabriel's kind eyes and said, "I am the Lord's servant. May it be to me as you have said."

After Gabriel left her, Mary stood in silence for a few moments and then made her way once more to the roof and gazed up to heaven. Exhausted, excited, and exuberant all at the same time, she collapsed to her knees, her arms too weak to raise, and she once more emphasized the words through a whisper: "I trust you, oh God."

Somewhere in the silence, she thought she heard a whisper return on the wind, "And I trust you, my child."

Scriptural Account

LUKE 1:26-38

In the sixth month [of Elizabeth's pregnancy], God sent the angel Gabriel to Nazareth, a town in Galilee, to a virgin pledged to be married to a man named Joseph, a descendant of David. The virgin's name was Mary. The angel went to her and said, "Greetings, you who are highly favored! The Lord is with you."

Mary was greatly troubled at his words and wondered what kind of greeting this might be. But the angel said to her, "Do not be afraid, Mary, you have found favor with God. You will be with child and give birth to a son, and you are to give him the name Jesus. He will be great and will be called the Son of the Most High. The Lord God will give him the throne of his father David, and he will reign over the house of Jacob for ever; his kingdom will never end."

"How will this be," Mary asked the angel, "since I am a virgin?"

The angel answered, "The Holy Spirit will come upon you, and the power of the Most High will overshadow you. So the holy one to be born will be called the Son of God. Even Elizabeth your relative is going to have a child in her old age, and she who was said to be barren is in her sixth month. For nothing is impossible with God."

"I am the Lord's servant," Mary answered, "May it be to me as you have said." Then the angel left her.

3

STRENGTHENED
BY AN ANGEL

Introduction

Have you ever noticed that divine things happen at just the right time. The Scriptures echo this sentiment when we are told, "*At just the right time Christ died for the ungodly.*" God still works that way. He always has and always will. He knows our every need and he delivers at the perfect time, with a perfect message, and often with an unexpected messenger. You hear it in the divine story of heavenly visitations during the most celebrated event in history. At the heart of this story is a promise that brings strength when you feel weak, warmth when you feel alone, and hope when days are dark. This promise was delivered from the tongues of angels to the fearful ears of Mary, Joseph, and the shepherds. And if you listen carefully, you will hear it in the soft cries of an infant lying in a manger. The promise is for you, too. Are you ready? Here it is: *Do not fear; God is here.* Say it to yourself until its truth echoes into your very soul.

Have you learned some devastating news that has caused you to despair? *Do not fear; God is here.* Do you face some uncertainties in the near future? *Do not fear; God is here.* He knows your heartaches, headaches, pains, and pressures. They all came to rest in his hands, feet, and side. He came to heal the leper, raise the paralytic, and open the blind eyes of the beggar. There is no storm his presence cannot calm.

Prepare yourself for the valleys and peaks ahead by standing on the summit of God's assurance of strength—breathing in the fragrance of God's presence and promises. Write down your past troubles and your fears for your future, and present them to God in prayer. Place them in a box, wrap them up, and write on the tag: *Do not fear; God is here.* Search through the scriptures; find all the "do not be afraid" passages, and read one a day through the month. You should never face tomorrow until you are filled with God's promise for today.

Yes, God shows up at just the right time leading us into uncertainties with assurance that whatever we encounter, we can safely say, "Do not fear; God is here."

Strengthened by an Angel

Joseph's mood mirrored the darkening sky as he trudged down the familiar, dusty streets of Nazareth toward his carpentry shop. A clutter of noises filled the air: shopkeepers closing their stores, scampering feet responding to the harmonizing calls of moms from a hundred doorways, and the last bit of laughter, gossip, and good-nights, which signaled the end of a busy day in the small town. Joseph usually stopped to listen to this symphony of sound, but tonight he heard nothing but his own confused thoughts.

Under normal circumstances, he would be heading home to wash off the sawdust and wood shavings that had accumulated in his beard and clothes through the day. But he knew he would not be going home this evening or even later tonight. The news he had just received from the woman he was soon to marry had left him feeling haunted, hurt, and helpless; and there was only one place he could go to think.

Some men get drunk after receiving such news, others try to act as though they never received it at all, and still others immerse themselves in their work. Joseph was one of those who did the latter. As he pulled the door of his shop open and heard the familiar creak of the hinges, he suddenly relived the shock of hearing Mary say the words— "I'm going to have a baby."

Her insistence that she had not been with another man rang in his ears. He stopped just outside the door and placed his hand over his abdomen, squeezing tightly, bending slightly, trying to alleviate the dull aching sensation and the coming nausea. The sick feeling was not for him, but for her.

He could easily put up with the off-color remarks, snickers, and whispers of small-town men and women who would soon receive this bit of big-time gossip, but what about her? It would destroy this beautifully spiritual woman he had learned to love so deeply. Before he could stop the words, they exploded from deep within him. "What am I going to do?" he moaned.

Over the next few hours, Joseph completed a massive, strong table that he had begun three days earlier for the town butcher, and the two chairs he had promised a widow down the street. Usually, this work would take the slow but sure carpenter three days to complete. But as his mind raced for a solution to his dilemma, so did his masterful and strong hands. As he thought about Mary's radiant smile and sweet spirit, his first inclination was to just go ahead and marry her. However, the chance of Mary's pregnancy being discovered and the ominous threat of her being stoned for adultery quickly cleared that idea from his mind. At midnight, as he was sweeping up the last bit of shavings and sawdust, he suddenly stopped and said out loud to himself, "That's it; that's what I'll do. I'll dismiss her quietly and get her out of town. With all the divorces going on today, her abrupt departure will feed a short-lived firestorm of gossip, and then it will be over and she will be safe. She can move to a new town where no one will know we hadn't yet married, and she can get on with her life. Being known as a divorcee is better than being stoned for adultery. That's it; that's it."

Relieved to finally have a plan, Joseph sat down, picked up a wineskin, and drank deeply from it. Suddenly, the fatigue from work and worry set in, and he decided to lay his head down on a bench and rest before tackling a couple of projects he was finishing for his own house. Sleep came quickly.

In the depths of sleep, Joseph suddenly sensed a cool breeze brushing his cheek, and the refreshing fragrance of the ocean mingled with the sweetness of lilacs filled his nostrils. But what he was most aware of was the song. It was the most beautiful song he had ever heard, and the soothing words filled his soul with assurance and security. Feeling an arm around him, he turned in his dream and looked directly into the broad smile of an angel. Joseph immediately fell to his knees. Without hesitation the angel knelt in front of him. Joseph was filled with fright at the sight of his massive arms and broad flowing wings, but as the angel placed his hands on Joseph's shoulders, he spoke in a tone that erased all of Joseph's fears. "Joseph son of David, do not be afraid to take Mary home as your wife, because the child she bears will save his people from their sins."

At this, the angel stood, spread his enormous wings, and flew from Joseph's presence. As soon as the angel was out of sight, Joseph woke from his dream. The first rays of light had just entered the room and were slowly making their way toward Joseph. He was amazingly alert—almost as if he had never been asleep—and he could still sense the fragrance of lilacs on the wind.

He slowly arose from his seat, went to the window that faced the rising sun, and knelt with his hands lifted high. With tears streaming from his eyes, flowing down his cheeks, and into his dark beard, he spoke in a whisper, "I worship you, oh Lord; I worship you. I pledge my strength, my soul, and my life to you. Your praise will be on my lips and in my heart forever, for you have blessed this lowly servant with riches of heaven." As he began to rise, he hesitated and sank once more to his knees and said with emphasis, "Thank you for my Mary, Lord. I will love her and the child you have placed within her with a fiercely protective love. The kind of love you have for me."

As he ended his prayer, he stood and bounded from his shop singing the song he had heard in his dream. He ran quickly to Mary's house where he found her sweeping her doorway. Her eyes were swollen and red from a night of weeping for the man she loved. He took the broom from her hands and softly said, "Mary, a heavenly messenger gave me the most welcome news of my life last night. And I have pledged to God that I will love you and the child he has given us, just as he has loved me."

Mary's expression turned from sadness to astonishment when Joseph said "us." Her knees buckled as she felt released from the fear of facing the future without Joseph, and she softly said, "You said 'us.'"

With the warmest smile she had ever seen on Joseph's face, he replied slowly and strongly, "Yes, us."

Joseph lifted her to her feet, and as they made their way down the busy street, he told her all about the angel and taught her his newly learned heavenly tune while he brushed the night's sawdust and wood shavings from his beard and off of his cloths.

Scriptural Account
MATTHEW 1:18-24

This is how the birth of Jesus Christ came about: His mother Mary was pledged to be married to Joseph, but before they came together, she was found to be with child through the Holy Spirit. Because Joseph her husband was a righteous man and did not want to expose her to public disgrace, he had in mind to divorce her quietly.

But after he had considered this, an angel of the Lord appeared to him in a dream and said, "Joseph son of David, do not be afraid to take Mary home as your wife, because what is conceived in her is from the Holy Spirit. She will give birth to a son, and you are to give him the name Jesus, because he will save his people from their sins."

All this took place to fulfill what the Lord had said through the prophet: "The virgin will be with child and will give birth to a son, and they will call him Immanuel"—which means, "God with us."

When Joseph woke up, he did what the angel of the Lord had commanded him and took Mary home as his wife.

4

ANGEL OF JOY

Introduction

 You may not know it, but you have in your possession treasures of immeasurable worth. You didn't buy them with a check or credit card—you couldn't have afforded them if you'd tried, and they're not for sale if you could. Even though they are more precious than all the possessions you've accumulated throughout your whole life, you may be allowing them to gather dust in a dark corner of your mind. These treasures were given to you as a gift, a blessing, and if you look with spiritual eyes, you'll see them as explosions of brilliant color on the canvas of your life.

I speak of holy moments, experiences you have witnessed or participated in that were so rich with meaning that your life would be dull and destitute without them. Perhaps one such moment was an act of kindness that led to a lifelong friendship, a date that led to matrimony, or a kiss on the cheek of a precious infant. Maybe you've experienced the brush of a tiny, inquisitive hand against your own, or a view of God's creation that affirmed a wavering faith. Possibly a message of joy was delivered to your heart on a lonely night from the loving God who knew you needed assurance.

Whatever holy moments you've experienced, now is the time to throw open the windows of your mind and allow the light to shine on those vibrant moments. Pour a cup of coffee and find the photo album. Sit on the porch with someone special and open the door to the storage closet of you mind. Wipe the dust from their memory, polish them up, and let the beauty and wonder of heaven's gifts impact today, tomorrow, and the rest of your life.

Angel of Joy

The absolute silence echoed in Hallel's ears. No one spoke a word; not a wing fluttered. Even more amazing, the sound of praise and worship that continually echoed through the halls of heaven had ceased. The angel could not remember another time like it; heaven was silent. Hallel would never have believed there would be a time when he was not leading a heavenly host in a vast assortment of songs and choruses. As the angel of praise, he was ordained to lead heaven in perpetual adulation and ceaseless song, and he carried out his duties joyfully.

The Father had gifted him with a clear, inviting voice, which emboldened even the most timid angel to join the worship with wholehearted enthusiasm. His face beamed with a constant smile. Even in this uncommon and rather uncomfortable silence, his eyes blazed with anticipation as he thought about the sequence of events that had led to this moment and the miracle that was about to unfold. All of heaven and earth had looked forward to the coming occurrence since the Father had formed humans in his image.

Hallel had been preparing songs of praise for the anticipated event when Gabriel had delivered the unsettling message. If the request had not come directly from Gabriel, Hallel would have thought it a deception from Lucifer or one of his cohorts. But the excitement in Gabriel's voice and the urgent expression on his face punctuated his plea with authenticity. Gabriel instructed him to leave his perch of praise and fly immediately to the throne room of Almighty God.

Putting Micah, his assistant, in charge of the heavenly chorus, Hallel flew to his meeting with lightning speed. He entered the glorious presence of the Father and covered his face with his wings as he knelt before God, saying, "Glory be to you, almighty God. How may I serve you?"

With a voice as beautiful as a comforting wind, the Father spoke, "Hallel, you have served me well, from the beginning until now. Your brilliant songs of praise have been heard from the depths of the earth to the farthest reaches of the heavenlies. I know you may be confused by my instructions; however, I am confident you will carry them out as I ask, for you follow me out of love.

"Very soon, the most wonderful incident of all measured time will take place on earth. You know the event I speak of?"

"Yes, my Lord. I was preparing praises for the birth when you called."

With a broad smile, the Father continued, "Gather your heavenly host and prepare to go where my Son will be born. You are to arrive in Bethlehem on the day of the birth. But when you get there, do not make a sound; no songs, no praise, no speech. You are to be completely silent."

A baffled look swept Hallel's face. His wings trembled, "No songs of worship?" he asked. The Father affirmed, "None."

"But Lord," Hallel boldly protested, "I find it difficult to refrain from breaking into praise just being in your presence this short time. How can I keep the whole host, let alone myself, quiet in anticipation of your Son's birth?"

The Father's eyes brightened even more, "Hallel, my Son's birth will be a holy occurrence that will never be repeated. The future of the world revolves around the birth of my Son. Hearts will be healed, the dead will be raised, fear will be defeated, and my enemy Satan will no longer be able to steal the joy of my children. Love that has grown stale will be renewed, fullness will replace emptiness, and dreams will become reality. In honor of this sacred moment, the night shall be silent when my Son enters the world. Go in silence and witness this sacred event with the heavenly host nearby. When you hear the first cry from the lips of the infant and see the first quiver of his lips, gather your host and deliver the message of joy that the Savior is born."

Immediately Hallel asked, "Who shall receive this wonderful announcement? Which king or ruler have you chosen to hear?"

"No dignitary is worthy of his news. Go to the faithful, the poor, and the weak. Go first to the shepherds outside the city of Bethlehem who raise my sacrificial lambs. They shall hear the news first because my Son will be both sheep and shepherd for my people." As the Father spoke, he held out a book, "When you make the announcement, sing this song. Sing it so that it fills heaven and earth and the caverns of hell with the announcement that victory belongs to the Father and his children."

Hallel looked at the book, smiled with appreciation, and turned, saying, "Your will be done, my Lord and my God."

Hallel immediately gathered his host from their stations across the heavens, and they sang as they made their way to the little town of Bethlehem. Since the setting of earth's sun until now, not a word had been uttered by any heavenly being, and the night was silent as never before. As the host waited in the distance, Hallel posted himself in the stable with Mary and Joseph, awaiting his signal. Unseen, he paced back and forth with Joseph. Hallel winced at the virgin's birth pains, prayed for her relief, and stared in amazement at the first sight of the child's head. As Joseph spoke words of encouragement to Mary, Hallel found himself cheering her on as well, "That's it Mary. You can do it. Just a little longer."

Then Hallel heard it; the soft cry that was quickly quieted at Mary's breast. Hallel sprang up, flexed his mighty wings, and flew to the waiting host. He wanted to shout for joy to the whole world, but he knew the first words were for the shepherds. He motioned to the host to follow him to the nearby fields. There he found the chosen shepherds tending their sheep. He watched for a moment and thought to himself. *These shepherds have no idea that their lives are about to be changed forever.* Instantly, he appeared to them in a flash of glory. The shepherds ran backwards in fear, but Hallel approached them, glowing with delight. "Do not be afraid. I bring you good news of great joy that will be for all the people." As he spoke, they cautiously moved closer, drawn by his warm smile and inviting voice. "Today in the town of David a Savior has been born to you; he is Christ the Lord." The shepherds knelt at the sound of the news. "This will be a sign to you: you will find a baby wrapped in cloths and lying in a manger." Hallel turned and commanded, "Sing the song the Lord has given us," and the heavenly host appeared and filled the silent night with praise. Hallel joined the throng and together they sang, "Glory to God in the highest, and on earth peace to men on whom his favor rests." They sang it again and again, louder with each refrain. The shepherds joined the singing with all their hearts and danced around the flock. As the host retreated, the song hung in the air, a sweet incense of praise.

Hallel followed the shepherds into the town where they found the Savior, just as he had told them. As they knelt in wonder, he knelt invisibly with them, placing his wings around them, and quietly sang again, "Glory to God in the highest, and on earth peace to men on whom his favor rests."

SECTION TWO

BELIEVE

5

A BRUSH WITH ANGELS

Introduction

Here is a question for you. You may be inspired to answer immediately, or you may want to contemplate it awhile. Feel free to take as much time as you need. Are you ready? *Have you ever experienced a hug from heaven?* Have you ever felt the brush of an angel wing that changed your course, sensed a small voice that sent you on an unplanned mission, or experienced a warm embrace of assurance from an unexpected source? Has a much-needed parcel been received just when it could help the most, or has a divine message arrived that filled your drained heart to overflowing with the love of God?

If so, you have most certainly experienced a hug from heaven. And what exactly do these experiences mean? The same thing that God has been trying to tell us since he sent a bear hug from heaven in the form of an infant lying in a manger, surrounded by a proud mom and dad and some very surprised shepherds. Hugs from heaven remind you that you are not alone and that God knows what you need.

So what do you do with these hugs from heaven? Let the warmth of their truth live in your heart every day so that when the cold winds of doubt or fear blow on your life (and they will), you can rest assured that there is a strong and caring hand leading you home.

Oh, and don't be surprised if someday, somewhere, you find yourself delivering a hug from heaven to someone else. You'll probably look just as surprised as the shepherds.

A Brush with Angels

Seth's chest swelled as he inhaled deeply, enjoying the sweet mixture of fragrant vegetation and salt sea, both of which had drifted to Bethlehem on a gentle southwest wind. It was a welcome scent after spending a grueling day tending his herd of dust-raising, grass-eating, musty-smelling sheep. It was at this time of night, every night, while their herds slept, that five of the shepherds from the surrounding fields came together and conversed about family, shepherding, money, politics, and anything else that came to mind. All five of them—Seth, Eli, Jonathan, Asa, and Matthan—were third-generation shepherds. Although most of the citizenry of Israel looked down on shepherding because it was considered filthy and alienating work, those who lived in the cities were totally reliant on the shepherds to supply the sacrifices they were offered to God. These five men were keenly aware of the disdain the locals felt for them, and their shared estrangement created and sustained a loyal bond of kinship between them. Not only were they bound together by their ostracism, but they also shared a profound awareness of their responsibility to supply the sacrificial lambs for Israel's worship of Almighty God.

Seth lifted a new wineskin and drank deeply from it and then passed it to his companions. Each took his turn and savored the wonderful flavor as the wine washed away the day's dust that had accumulated in their throats. Jonathan, the youngest of the group, with dark hair and skin and brilliantly bright eyes, spoke first: "Have any of you noticed the silence in the air tonight? Even the ships are still. I haven't heard a sound from any of them all evening." His eyes darted back and forth over the herd, looking and listening for movement.

Seth, the oldest in both age and appearance, nearly whispered, "The silence feels almost reverent, as if the world were waiting for something to happen." Eli, Asa, and

Matthan nodded and mumbled their agreement as they ran their fingers through their chest-length beards.

Matthan felt a shiver race through him and attempted to change the subject. "Have any of you heard the news that is spreading all over Judea about the priest Zechariah?" The others exchanged puzzled expressions and shook their heads.

"What news, brother?" Eli asked.

"Well, no one can explain it, but his wife Elizabeth was barren."

"What's so interesting about that?" Seth quickly chided.

"Let me finish the story, Seth," said Matthan as he playfully pushed Seth off the stone he was sitting on. Matthan started again, "Listen, his wife was barren until he went into the temple of the Lord. According to him, an angel was standing at the right side of the altar of incense."

Jonathan's eyes were wide open, pleading with Matthan to continue, and he asked, "You mean a real angel from heaven?"

"Yes—a real angel," Matthan answered confidently.

"He had to be making that up," scoffed Eli.

"Well, listen to this," continued Matthan. "The angel told him that his wife would have the son they had been praying and begging God for and that this child would bring people back to God and prepare them for the coming of the Lord. When Zechariah demonstrated his doubt that such a thing could actually happen, the angel silenced his tongue. When the priest walked out of the temple, he couldn't make a sound."

"What happened next?" Jonathan begged.

"Well, after he went home, sure enough, his wife soon became pregnant, and she had a son just three months ago. And it wasn't until Zechariah gave him the name John, like the angel told him to do, that he could finally talk again."

Eli said aloud what the others were thinking, "What could all this mean?"

But Seth—the only doubter in the group—cynically mocked, "Angels from heaven—I don't believe it!"

Just as Seth was closing his mouth, an angel of the Lord appeared out of nowhere and the glory of the Lord shone all around them. The five frightened shepherds jumped up and ran toward the hills. But as he was running, Seth stumbled and fell to the ground; he lay frozen in fear. Then the angel picked Seth up and spoke to them all with a calming voice, beckoning them to return, "Do not be afraid. I bring you good news of great joy that will be for all the people."

A stunned Jonathan leaned over to Eli and in a trembling voice said, "Do you think he will silence our tongues too?"

Eli nervously replied, "Brother, I just hope to get out of this with my life—I don't care about my tongue!"

The angel smiled and continued in a soothing voice. The shepherds began to calm. "Today in the town of David a Savior has been born to you; he is Christ the Lord. This will be a sign to you: you will find a baby wrapped in cloths and lying in a manger."

Suddenly, the heavens were filled with angels, and they were praising God with a song. The shepherds—now assured they were in no danger and overjoyed by the news—joined in the song and began dancing under the host of angels. Then, as the song echoed in the night, the angels left them.

With the night still once again, all that could be heard was the panting of the shepherds. They looked at each other, then embraced and danced delightedly. "What do we do now?" they asked in unison.

"Let's go to Bethlehem and see this thing that has happened, which the Lord has told us about," said Seth. So they hurried off and found Mary and Joseph, and the baby who was lying in the manger. They timidly approached the couple and the sleeping baby. But their shyness evaporated at Mary and Joseph's radiant faces, and they excitedly relayed what had happened and why they had come.

Asa spoke up after their story had been told and said, "I know this must sound unbelievable to the two of you."

But Joseph and Mary just looked at each other and smiled. "Strangely enough," Joseph said, "it isn't hard to believe at all."

Haltingly, Seth asked Mary, "Could I touch the head of my Lord?"

Without saying a word, Mary lifted the cover, exposing the head of the child. One by one, each shepherd came forward, placed a hand on Jesus' head, and blessed him. Tears ran down weathered cheeks that had not felt the wet warmth for years.

When they had seen him, they spread the word concerning what had been told them about this child, and all who heard it were amazed at what the shepherds said to them. The shepherds returned, glorifying and praising God for all the things they had heard and seen, which were just as they had been told.

After that sacred night, the five shepherds continued to meet in the fields while their sheep slept. They still spoke of family and shepherding, but mostly they spoke about the goodness of the God they served. He had sent a special message to lowly shepherds about a royal birth. They, of all people, had been among the first to hear the announcement, delivered by angels. Of all people, they had heard the angelic host sing a heavenly song of hope. Of all people on earth, they had been among the first to see the Savior, who himself would be both shepherd and sheep for the world.

No one in Bethlehem ever looked down on shepherding again.

Scriptural Account

LUKE 2: 8-20

And there were shepherds living out in the fields nearby, keeping watching over their flocks at night. An angel of the Lord appeared to them, and the glory of the Lord shone around them, and they were terrified. But the angel said to them, "Do not be afraid. I bring you good news of great joy that will be for all the people. Today in the town of David a Savior has been born to you; he is Christ the Lord. This will be a sign to you: You will find a baby wrapped in cloths and lying in a manger."

Suddenly a great company of the heavenly host appeared with the angel, praising God and saying, "Glory to God in the highest, and on earth peace to men on whom his favor rests."

When the angels had left them and gone into heaven, the shepherds said to one another, "Let's go to Bethlehem and see this thing that has happened, which the Lord has told us about."

So they hurried off and found Mary and Joseph, and the baby, who was lying in the manger. When they had seen him, they spread the word concerning what had been told them about this child, and all who heard it were amazed at what the shepherds said to them. Bur Mary treasured up all these things and pondered them in her heart. The shepherds returned, glorifying and praising God for all the things they had heard and seen, which were just as they had been told.

6

Mary's Song

Introduction

It happens every year at some point. It can happen at the first of the year when you are making resolutions you will forget, or perhaps after a long winter that is consumed with busy activity and worry. Some come to this point after a busy summer and going into a fall that is full of fiery colors. You say to yourself, "I'm going to enjoy my life and stop getting caught up in the rat race." But before you know it, you've stepped on the accelerator of life and the pedal stays on the floor until you have another "awakening." Your thoughts are filled with worries about work, bills, kids, the future, and on and on it goes. You spend endless hours consumed with items and events you can't control and suddenly you realize you are under their control.

Then you stop and ask yourself, "Is this what life is meant to be?" Where did that childlike wonder and expectation that should remain a part of you go? Your growing list of responsibilities tightened your schedule and tempered your imagination. Endless waves of worry eroded your hopeful heart. In other words, you grew up, gained speed, and gave in to what the world calls the "the life of stress." So how can you rediscover that expectant heart you once had for life? What can you do to uncover the beauty and innocence that was once part of your daily existence?

You can renew your belief in what God did two thousand years ago. You can remember that the reason you have hope, purpose, and promise lies in the constant realization that you are loved and cared for by the One who can take care of everything, and in fact has already handled the largest problem you face—he took away the fear of death.

The Creator of the universe was cradled in the hands of a carpenter. The Son of the Most High was sustained by a mother's milk. The Son of a carpenter faced life head on and went through everything you could possibly experience and finally died on a cross, because God wanted you to have peace.

So slow down your pace and ponder the enormous love that God has for you. Spend less money and more time with those you love. Read Scripture and share with loved ones what you learn. Remember what was said of a virgin girl in need of assurance: "Blessed is she who has believed." And so are you.

Mary's Song

Mary arose with the rich smell of spring rain filling her small room. She went to her window and opened her eyes wide as if to allow a full measure of morning light into her waking body. She had slept in complete peace and security after her joyful meeting with Joseph, and today was a day she looked forward to with eager anticipation. She would hurry to see her cousin Elizabeth and tell her all the amazing and wonderful events that had happened and that were filling her heart.

Mary backed away from the window and knelt so that the sun, showing through the clearing sky, shone directly on her face. "My God, oh holy God, you are my strength, my hope, and my courage. You fill the morning with your sweet breath as the fragrance of heaven wakes the earth, and you have filled me with your child. So much of what you have given me remains a mystery, but as this child grows, so does my love for you. Help me as I share this mystery with Elizabeth and help her understand not only what you have done for me, but also what you have done for her, as the angel told me." Although Mary didn't really know how God could help her relay to Elizabeth this astonishing news, she knew he would.

As she stood, she looked down at her midsection and ran her opened hand over her abdomen. Even though the young Mary still felt some apprehension about the miracle birth, she found herself wishing she were showing more. She spoke lovingly, sweetly, to the invisible, heaven-sent child who was taking form inside her. "What will you look like, little one? Will you be different from other children?" She let out a small laugh as she said, "Of course you will; you will be the most beautiful child ever born. People will stop me and say, 'What a beautiful child you have—a real gift of God!'" Then she bent her head toward her belly and whispered—as if she were sharing a secret with her infant— "Little will they know how right they are."

Mary continued to speak affectionately to the divine life within her as she dressed quickly and set out for the hill country of Judah, where Elizabeth and Zechariah lived.

As she crossed over the last hill before entering the small town that was the home of her beloved relatives, she paused. Mary especially cherished this country at sunset. A bright orange glow radiated from the surrounding hills as they reflected the setting sun's last barrage of light before giving way to darkness. She took this opportunity to carefully rehearse the words she had chosen to say to Elizabeth in explaining the angel's visit and the miracle child she was carrying. She softly prayed, "Please help her understand, my God." Little did she know she would never get the chance to recite the lines she had practiced so diligently.

Elizabeth brushed an errant strand of thick, graying hair back into place as she stood over the remnants of the meal she and her husband had shared. It had been a silent supper for Zechariah, as had all the meals since the angel had silenced his tongue for doubting God's power to give him a child. However, Elizabeth filled these moments with her excited one-sided conversations about the baby's coming and the plans she had. Zechariah would just smile and nod at this precious Elizabeth's joy. Throughout her barren years, Zechariah had ached over the whispered insults of neighbors and Elizabeth's self-inflicted shame. But her joy at the coming event took much of the sting out of his punishment.

As Elizabeth prepared to stack the dishes, she heard Mary enter the door and call out her name. As soon as she heard Mary's voice, something extraordinary happened that surprised them both. The baby within Elizabeth became so active she could hardly remain on her feet. She held on to her chair and bent at the waist until the infant calmed. She was then filled with the Holy Spirit, and in a loud voice, she exclaimed: "Blessed are you among women, and blessed is the child you will bear! But why am I so favored, that the mother of my Lord should come to me? As soon as the sound of your greeting reached my ears, the baby in my womb leaped for joy."

Mary's eyes opened wide, tears streamed down her cheeks, and her hand rushed to cover her mouth which was open in utter amazement. God had delivered the message of her pregnancy for her. She hadn't had to utter a word. In shock, she whispered to herself, "You know; you know."

Elizabeth moved to Mary, pulled her close, and like a calming mother, laid Mary's head on her shoulder and swayed from side to side. She then delivered the unexpected message from God to his beloved Mary. Although it came in the form of Elizabeth's soft voice, Mary knew that it originated in heaven and that it held a very intentional purpose. It was said slowly and deliberately so that it would not need to be repeated, "Blessed is she who has believed that what the Lord has said to her will be accomplished!"

As soon as those words reached Mary's heart, she nearly collapsed in awe as she fully understood how much God loved her. It seemed that all the remaining fear and apprehension at the coming events had been washed away by this one soothing sentence, and she was keenly aware of the impact the life within her would have on the coming generations. She lowered her head to the floor, and as Elizabeth brushed her hand over her hair, Mary continued her day as she had begun it: "My soul glorifies the Lord and my spirit rejoices in God my Savior, for he has been mindful of the humble state of his servant. From now on all generations will call me blessed, for the Mighty One has done great things for me—holy is his name. His mercy extends to those who fear him, from generation to generation. He has performed mighty deeds with his arm; he has scattered those who are proud in their inmost thoughts. He has brought down rulers from their thrones but has lifted up the humble. He has filled the hungry with good things but has sent the rich away empty. He has helped his servant Israel, remembering to be merciful to Abraham and his descendants forever, even as he said to our fathers."

When Mary finished her prayer, she and Elizabeth arose together. They walked slowly to the table, arm in arm, as Mary excitedly told Elizabeth all that had happened and all that was filling her heart. Mary stayed with Elizabeth for about three months and then returned home. She felt no more fear from that day forward, and all of heaven was pleased.

Scriptural Account

LUKE 1:39-50

At that time Mary got ready and hurried to a town in the hill country of Judea, where she entered Zechariah's home and greeted Elizabeth. When Elizabeth heard Mary's greeting, the baby leaped in her womb, and Elizabeth was filled with the Holy Spirit. In a loud voice she exclaimed: "Blessed are you among women, and blessed is the child you will bear! But why am I so favored, that the mother of my Lord should come to me? As soon as the sound of your greeting reached my ears, the baby in my womb leaped for joy. Blessed is she who has believed that what the Lord has said to her will be accomplished!"

And Mary said:
"My soul glorifies the Lord
and my spirit rejoices in God my Savior,
for he has been mindful
of the humble state of his servant.
From now on all generations will call me blessed,
for the Mighty One has done great things for me—
holy is his name.
His mercy extends to those who fear him,
from generation to generation."

7

GUIDED BY GOD

Introduction

There is one question that you are asked more than you have ever realized. Listen for it and you will hear it from friends, family, coworkers, and neighbors, and everyone who asks will genuinely want to know the answer. You will hear the question in various forms and with different words, but it will come frequently. The question always has to do with what you have planned for the future. If you are a student you will hear it in the form of a question like this, "What are you doing after you graduate?" Or perhaps, "Where are you going to college?"

If you are going on vacation you will be asked, "Where are you going and what are you going to do while you are there?" And the question keeps coming, "What are you going to do this weekend?" Or you may be asked, "What's up tomorrow, the next day; are you going here, are you going there?"

The amazing thing is that you will probably be able to answer these questions with amazing detail, and those you ask will be able to do the same. Why? Because we like to know where we are going and what we are doing. The fact is we do know what we are doing tomorrow, and over the weekend. We do have our vacation planned and we have a pretty good idea what we are going to do once we get there. We like to make plans and try to stick to them, don't we? There is nothing wrong with that is there? No! With one word of caution: Go ahead and make your plans, mark your calendar, map out your course, make a detailed list, prepare for visits with friends and family, and try to stick with it. But you might add this to your cell phone appointments, or your calendar if you still keep one, or your day timer if you still have one. Just make a note that reminds you: "Leave room for God's plans."

The most rewarding experiences of our lives can come when we free our schedules and open our eyes to the unexpected surprises of a loving God. You might be on the way to the grocery store when you meet a hungry soul, or on your way to visit a neighbor when you run into a lonely heart. You may go to a party and encounter a stranger who desperately needs a word of encouragement. These divine moments cannot be planned or charted; they just happen. And you don't want to miss a single one, because these unplanned encounters may just change history.

God planned it that way.

Guided by God

Mary's plans for the arrival of her baby had not included this hot, dusty, three-day journey to Bethlehem. When Caesar Augustus had issued the decree that every man must go to his hometown to be counted in a census, Joseph had quickly but skillfully built a special seat for Mary in his carpentry wagon. Suspended by rope, the seat would absorb some of the shock of the rough terrain they would cover on the way to his hometown of Bethlehem.

Mary had wanted badly to have the baby in Nazareth in familiar surroundings, but with every mile of the bumpy road, the rumblings of the child served as warning that she might not make it back to her beloved town for the blessed event.

Joseph was well aware of Mary's discomfort, and though she never complained, he sensed that the time was upon them. He attempted to take her mind off the baby by filling the hours with tales of his childhood in Bethlehem. Mary laughed at his antics, and for a short time they relieved her concern. But there weren't enough stories to tell, and there were too many miles ahead. When Joseph ran out of stories to distract her, he noticed that she totally immersed herself in prayer.

In the heat of the afternoon of the third day, Joseph thought it would be wise to stop before the last push into Bethlehem. He built a covering with a cloth attached to stilts, which he stuck deep in the dirt, so they could rest in the cool of some shade. He knelt beside Mary and watched her gently massage her midsection. He looked into her beautiful, deep eyes and said, "We didn't plan for this, did we?"

She smiled shyly, running her soft fingers across Joseph's weathered brow, and gently replied, "No, and you didn't plan to marry a pregnant virgin, and I didn't plan to have a child planted in me by the hand of God." Then she gazed at the bright blue sky and said, "But Joseph, with every mile we travel I get a stronger and stronger sense that this is exactly what he has planned, and I trust him completely."

It was approaching dusk when they reached the Bethlehem city limits, and Mary couldn't help but notice the most beautiful sunset she had ever witnessed. At the thin line that separated earth and sky, a rainbow of yellows and reds hung above the earth, announcing the coming night. There were no clouds or wind, and the heavens were calm and peaceful. The streets were packed with weary travelers, shopkeepers, and street vendors all attempting to have their intentions served. After Joseph visited with several people who had already found shelter for the night, he knew that the only place to go was the town inn. Joseph arrived just as the innkeeper was renting the last room.

As the couple approached, the innkeeper reached out his hand, grasped Joseph's hand enthusiastically, and looked beyond Joseph at the very pregnant and obviously uncomfortable Mary. The man's name was Daniel—after the prophet—and the name represented the man's faith accurately. His hair was black with a few strands of gray, he was a bit heavyset, and his breathing was labored as he spoke. Under thick eyelids, his bright, joyful eyes betrayed a kind heart and warm spirit. His expression reflected sincere concern as Joseph explained their dilemma. "I'm sorry children," he said, "but I have nowhere for you to stay. I have even given up my own room for this throng of people; otherwise, I would gladly give it to you."

Upon seeing the dejection painted across Joseph's face, Daniel walked around the corner and then came back to them. "Listen, I know it probably isn't what you'd planned, but I have a stable in the back, and you can stay there free of charge."

Joseph searched Mary's face and found a strangely intuitive smile. "That will be fine, I guess," Joseph replied.

As Daniel led them to the stable, he stopped and said, "You know, I can hardly believe I offered you this place. I hadn't planned on anyone staying here tonight—especially someone who is going to have a baby—but oddly enough, it seems this is the way it's supposed to be." As he stepped into the stable, he began sweeping up a great mound of hay with his legs. Mary was touched as she noticed Daniel's breathing grow heavier from what, for him, was an enormous effort. When he had done all he could to prepare her bed, he turned to Mary and said, "I hope you sleep well, dear child. Do not hesitate to call on me for anything you need. May God bless you."

As Joseph and Daniel stood outside and talked for a minute more, Mary knelt in the straw where she would soon have her child and prayed, "My God, I know you have brought me here to have your Child. Now, this is just a stable; but once your Son enters, it will be the most beautiful place on earth—for that is how you've planned it. May I serve your will." With that, Mary prepared herself and a place in the straw for the coming of Jesus.

As the kind Daniel walked away, he repeated again and again, "If you need anything, children, don't hesitate to ask. I am not far away." He was true to his word and true in his heart to the young couple. Little did he know that he would be linked to the Christ forever in heaven and on earth, for that was the way God had planned it all along.

Scriptural Account

LUKE 2:1-7

In those days Caesar Augustus issued a decree that a census should be taken of the entire Roman world. . . . And everyone went to his own town to register.

So Joseph also went up from the town of Nazareth in Galilee to Judea, to Bethlehem the town of David, because he belonged to the house and line of David. He went there to register with Mary, who was pledged to be married to him and was expecting a child. While they were there, the time came for the baby to be born, and she gave birth to her firstborn, a son. She wrapped him in cloths and placed him in a manger, because there was no room for them in the inn.

8

Honored by God

Introduction

If I asked you to make a comprehensive list of words associated with God giving his Son for us, you would probably find the task quite simple. Words such as love, joy, peace, goodwill, sacrifice, and gift would pour from your lips with ease.

However, there is another word, perhaps less likely to make your list, that really should stand above all others. It is a word that forces us to examine the real meaning of God's gift much the way a jeweler peers into the depths of a precious stone to assess its value. For just as the sparkle of a precious gem begins within its core, every other glowing term used to describe heaven's visit to our world begins at the core of what God did for us. The word is *honored*. A little over two thousand years ago, God honored you and me with his presence. In light of the poverty, pain, and peril he knew he would face in our world, he could have chosen to stay home. Instead, he tore the curtains that separated the divine from the dishonored, blasted through the walls that divided perfection from the perverse, and broke down the doors that isolated true royalty from the rabble. And because it might be difficult for us to identify with him if he came to a palace or castle, he honored our simplicity by being born in a stable, through the womb of a teenager.

Take out your magnifying glass and look back at the scene of this event. Smell the musty odors of the stable; listen to the heavy breathing of a virgin who has just given birth to the Savior; view the face of a rough-handed carpenter who cradled our eternal destiny in his hands.

But above all, don't miss the infant. See the small body that traveled all the way from heaven. Hear him cry for his mother's milk. Feel the soft flesh of a newborn who came to save the world. And never, ever forget that you are the reason he came.

Every single day, we honor him for who he is. But he came and honored us with his presence because he knew what we could become.

Honored by God

It was almost midnight when Joseph stepped from the stable for a moment's rest as Mary's labor temporarily subsided. He rubbed his eyes with the palms of his hands and then ran his hands down the length of his beard. He vigorously pounded his chest and arms until he felt fully alert. The silence of the surrounding night was overwhelming. He looked up and down the barren streets and listened to the stillness.

Just a few hours before, people had crowded the streets with laughter, friendly conversation, tearful reunions, and political dialogue. He had thought to himself, then, that no one in these city streets—or for that matter, in the whole world—knew what wonderful miracle would soon take place inside this stable. Not just a miracle of new life, but also the miracle of a visitor from heaven who would somehow impact their world for eternity. Joseph didn't know exactly how, but he was keenly aware that not only his life, but the lives of all people everywhere were about to change.

At one point in the evening—when the full weight of this realization landed in his heart—he nearly jumped up and ran into the streets to tell anyone who would listen. But the cold water of logic doused his enthusiasm when he realized he didn't know what he would say. How could he explain that God had chosen Mary, a virgin, and himself, a poor carpenter, to bring his own special child into the world? Or that the blessed event was about to happen in a hay-filled, animal-housing stable? "Sure thing, Joseph," he said to himself with a laugh. "They would surely believe that, wouldn't they?"

Now, as he stood alone in the night, he stretched out his arms as wide as they would reach, took a deep breath, and looked up at the diamond-filled sky. The moonless night enhanced the glow of the stars so that they formed a blanket of brilliant light. He silently asked himself when he had last been so stunned by the sheer beauty of an Israel night.

The wonder of it all triggered something in Joseph. The joy of a future shared with his beloved Mary and this soon-to-be-born child, whom he would name Jesus, swept over him like a refreshing rain shower. He began to dance under the night sky and sang out in a loud voice, "What a blessed man you are, Joseph; what a blessed man you are." He stopped, arched his back, and spoke to the attentive stars, "Stars, shimmer like you have never shimmered before, because I will soon introduce you to my son, Jesus, and I want you to look your very best."

He turned to the quiet, empty streets of the city and cried out with pride and joy, "Bethlehem, my beloved Bethlehem, you have been the home of King David, and his mighty men. You have seen the greatest rulers of the world. But you have never seen anything like you will see tonight. Within your bosom is one being born who will make you worth more than if your buildings were covered in gold and your streets were lined with silver." As he heard Mary groan in the pains of childbirth, he whispered, "And there is a woman in our midst of whom neither you nor I are worthy." Suddenly, Mary's strained voice called out for Joseph, and he went in to help deliver the coming child.

After cutting the umbilical cord with his knife, Joseph carefully picked up the baby and cradled him in his arms. He ever-so-tenderly touched the soft skin of the infant, fearing that his rough hands would hurt the baby. Mary's face filled with pride as she watched her husband cuddle God's child. When Jesus began to whimper, Mary took him into her arms and wrapped him in strips of cloth and laid him down in the manger. Mary and Joseph looked into each other's eyes and smiled as they brushed the tears from each other's cheeks. "Jesus, meet Joseph," Mary said to her child. "And Joseph, meet Jesus."

Joseph responded playfully, "Where have you been, little Jesus? We've been waiting for you for so long." His words trailed off as he repeated soberly, ". . . for so long," again and again.

Joseph scooped the child up into his arms. "Mary, I have to introduce Jesus to someone; I'll be right back." With that, Joseph walked with deliberation and pride into the starry night. He looked up at the heavens and said, 'Jesus, meet all the stars of heaven. They are shimmering just for you. I told them you were coming, and they put on their very best lights—just for you." Then he turned Jesus toward the city and said, "Jesus meet Bethlehem. You have brought this old city great honor tonight. It is very proud you are here." He then brushed his lips against Jesus' forehead and said, "But most of all, you have honored me tonight, and I am very proud you are here."

Scripture Account
ISAIAH 9:6

For to us a child is born,
to us a son is given,
    and the government will be on his shoulders.
And he will be called
Wonderful Counselor, Mighty God,
Everlasting Father, Prince of Peace.

SECTION THREE

OVERCOME

9

COMFORTED BY AN ANGEL

Introduction

There is something you most definitely need to know. It is one of the most compelling of all truths. You may have already learned this truth while enduring hardship or struggling through the stormy torrents of this life. Once you know it, once you really become aware of it in the depths of your soul, you will never again look into the face of evil with fear or walk in darkness feeling lost and abandoned.

Look into a mirror and recite these words to the person you see: *You are not, nor will you ever be alone.* Say it again and allow the words to flow over you like a refreshing wind. *You are not, nor will you ever be alone.*

It is a simple message of comfort, but it is heavy with importance. God has eagerly heralded it in his Word since he formed our flesh and breathed life into our lungs. When you feel burdened by life's heaviest decisions and your knees begin to buckle under the weight, he says, "Come to me." When you hunger because the world's offerings have left you empty, he says, "Eat this bread and drink this cup." When you need encouragement to persevere past the pain of rejection or heartache, he reminds you that you have a great cloud of witnesses cheering you on. When failure and disappointment become your companions or loneliness threatens your faith, he says, "Never will I leave you, never will I forsake you." When Satan's lies of the Father's desertion make their way through the cracks of your faith, revisit the promise of our loving God: "Draw near to me and I will draw near to you." Move into his open arms as he wraps them around you gently and pulls you close. His smile says it all: *You are not, nor will you ever be alone.*

Comforted by an Angel

The bright colors of the rainbow in the distance presented a stark contrast to the sun-baked earth tones of the desert, especially where the two met on the thin line of the horizon. As the archangel Michael viewed the scene, he felt the same contrast within himself. He sensed the approaching end to the grueling confrontation between his previous superior and now nemesis, Lucifer, and the Messiah. He had savored the satisfaction of watching the Messiah defy the evil one's relentless stream of temptations during these nearly forty days. Yet he doubted that the roaring lion had retreated from the hunt.

As Jesus neared the end of his time in the desert he had called home for the last several weeks, he was drained and exhausted. The dual strain of fasting and standing firm against Satan had gravely affected his physical health. In a bare whisper, Jesus said to his Father, "I am so hungry and tired." As Michael watched the Son of Man stumble and nearly fall as his legs buckled beneath him, he asked the Father if he could now go and minister to Jesus. The angel was surprised by the answer. "No, not yet, Michael. The dragon isn't done with this battle, and neither is my Son."

No sooner had the Father finished speaking than Michael heard the familiar deep and raspy voice of Lucifer: "That's right Michael." The evil one hovered near Jesus' weary body as he spoke. "I am far from finished. Everything until now was meant simply to cripple, not to destroy. I am now ready to assault him with my most powerful temptations . . . while he is in his weakest state."

Michael quickly positioned himself between Jesus and Lucifer, saying, "I know well the tactics that caused the fall of Adam, Israel, David, and others. Remember, I was there. The Father's grace defeated you then, and his love for his children will defeat you now. Don't forget that I am nearby, eagerly awaiting the Father's command to move."

Suddenly, Satan made himself visible to Jesus, and his ugly guttural voice became sweet and soothing. "If you are the Son of God, tell these stones to become bread."

Even though Jesus' weakened body craved to do just as Satan suggested, his whisper-soft voice gained strength with every word as he answered, "It is written: 'Man does not live on bread alone, but in every word that comes from the mouth of God.'" At these words, an echo of cheers could be heard from the heavenlies.

The devil then took Jesus by the hand and led him to the holy city. Michael followed close behind, longing to be told he could move to the Messiah's aid. Satan stood with Jesus on the highest point of the temple and said with intimidating arrogance, "If you are the Son of God, throw yourself down. For it is written: 'He will command his angels concerning you, and they will lift you up in their hands, so that you will not strike your foot against a stone.'" He looked momentarily at Michael and bobbed his head as if to say, "Isn't that true, Michael?"

Jesus answered him with a clear voice, surprising in its strength, "It is also written: 'Do not put the Lord your God to the test.'" Again, as the words left the lips of Jesus, a wall of cheering filled the heavens and Michael smiled.

Next, the devil took Jesus to a high mountain and showed him all the kingdoms of the world and their splendor. With his long, elegant fingers, he pointed out the cities, palaces, and beautiful buildings. Then in a richly sincere voice, he said, "All this I will give you, if you will only bow down and worship me."

As Michael listened attentively to this latest temptation, he thought to himself, *You liar; only you would offer what you do not own.*

Jesus' eyes flashed with life and his back straightened. Without hesitation, he looked into the face of the devil and said, "Away from me, Satan! For it is written: 'Worship the Lord your God, and serve him only.'" The intensity with which Jesus spoke set Satan back on his heels. All traces of his smile vanished, and he covered his ears against the sea of praise and applause the angel host poured down upon the mountain. Suddenly, he turned and disappeared into a cloud of darkness as he spat his threats of return and ultimate victory.

With loud songs of adoration still filling the air like endless rolls of thunder, the Father spoke to Michael, "Quickly, send your angels to attend to my Son's needs." Immediately a score of angels descended and encircled Jesus, offering encouragement, embraces, food, and drink. Comforted and filled, the Messiah lay down to sleep. Michael flew to the sleeping form and placed Jesus' weary head in his lap. As he lovingly brushed his sweaty hair from his face, he said, "Sleep sweetly, O King—both God and man. We are so proud of you. Only heaven witnessed your courage and holiness today, but one day all the world will know of it. The evil one is not through with you yet. You will face him again, but the love of the Father and all of heaven will sustain you."

Scriptural Account
MATTHEW 4:1-11

Then Jesus was led by the Spirit into the desert to be tempted by the devil. After fasting forty days and forty nights, he was hungry. The tempter came to him and said, "If you are the Son of God, tell these stones to become bread."

Jesus answered, "It is written: 'Man does not live on bread alone, but on every word that comes from the mouth of God.'"

Then the devil took him to the holy city and had him stand on the highest point of the temple. "If you are the Son of God," he said, "throw yourself down. For it is written:

'He will command his angels concerning you,

and they will lift you up in their hands,

so that you will not strike your foot against a stone.'"

Jesus answered him, "it is also written: 'Do not put the Lord your God to the test.'"

Again, the devil took him to a very high mountain and showed him all the kingdoms of the world and their splendor. "All this I will give you," he said, "if you will bow down and worship me."

Jesus said to him, "Away from me, Satan! For it is written: 'Worship the Lord your God, and serve him only.'"

Then the devil left him, and angels came and attended him.

10

Believing the Impossible

Introduction

Would you describe yourself as a healer? Probably not, but that would be a great mistake. I know that your idea of a healer might be a skilled surgeon working to save a life with a scalpel in hand and a crack team of nurses gathered around. Maybe it's the family physician carefully listening to an ailing heart with a stethoscope and trained ears or looking at x-rays against the light with attentive eyes. Now you can add one more picture to the healing heroes in your mind. Yours!

Oh, you may never cut away some life-threatening cancer with a scalpel, but your friendship removes the heartache of loneliness. A warm embrace or tender touch from you is like a refreshing rain that washes through your friends and brings renewal. You may never listen through a stethoscope or scan x-rays, but your ears are attentive, listening carefully to your friend's concerns. And it seems that your eyes have been trained to see into the slumping soul and brittle spirit that needs encouraging and strengthening.

Yes, your touch, eyes, and ears are tools for healing, and you use them as skillfully as any surgeon or physician ever could. If you ever wonder how your friendship affects others, if you ever ask yourself whether your friendship is needed, remember the Great Physician who healed hearts, bodies, and lives without a single medical instrument. The power of his presence and his love was enough to make the unhealthy person whole. You resemble him.

Believing the Impossible

It was mid-afternoon, and Hannah felt the strength-sapping heat of the sun even more keenly than the other expectant people who lined the streets of Capernaum. A severely thin wrist appeared from under her cloak and ran across her gaunt face to wipe the beads of perspiration that had formed across her dark brow and petite nose. It was easy to see that at one time she had been radiantly attractive. However, high cheekbones and strikingly deep blue eyes were all that remained of her swiftly escaping beauty.

Twelve years earlier, Hannah had been a much-loved young girl with high hopes. And in this small community of Capernaum, her friends and family had even higher expectations. Everyone, including Hannah , was sure that she would marry well and have exceptionally beautiful children like herself. She lived what some had called a charmed life. All who knew her believed that God had personally touched her with his blessings. But something happened in her eighteenth year of life that no one could have predicted and, it seemed, no one was prepared for.

It began one afternoon while Hannah was helping her mother prepare for the evening meal. A knife slipped and sliced across her index finger. The bleeding was excessive, and all attempts to stop the flow were totally ineffective. It was not until several hours later that her mother finally began to see the blood clot and cease its relentless stream. The whole experience left her mother and father fearful. Not just for her health, but for what the community would think if they found out. No one would want anything to do with a young woman subject to bleeding. They watched her closely that night as she lay in her bed, shivering, pale, and weak from blood loss.

It happened again one day when she was with her friends and cut her foot on a sharp rock. The friends panicked because they couldn't stop the bleeding, and the news of Hannah's problem soon spread through the community like a cold wind. Icy stares and receptions greeted Hannah on the streets. One by one her friends deserted her, and there were absolutely no suitors to consider for marriage.

Over the next few years, she depleted her family's money, desperately going from physician to physician—each one promising a cure, each one claiming to have the knowledge to supply the healing she so hungered for, each on eagerly taking her money. She anxiously took their medicines and followed their instructions, but her continued bouts with bleeding took away her hope, leaving her weakened, helpless, and heartbroken. By her thirtieth birthday, she had stopped searching for cures and had surrendered to the forced exile placed on her by former friends and neighbors. There was no place in their hearts for a woman subject to bleeding, so she took a small dwelling on the outskirts of town and lived alone, waiting to die. That is, until now.

For the past several days, her parents had been telling her about a man named Jesus. He was a true friend of the hurting, they told her. In fact, they said, "He is a true friend to anyone who comes to him." They had heard him speak on a mount just north of Capernaum, and his teaching was like pure water cascading into the hearts of all those who were there. "But that was just the beginning," her mother told her. "As Jesus walked down from the mountainside, a man with leprosy appeared. Everyone started backing away when they saw the leper come and kneel before Jesus."

"Did Jesus push him away?" Hannah eagerly asked.

"No, Hannah. He reached out his hand and touched the man and said, 'Be clean.'"

"What happened next?" Hannah's voice and expression wore the excitement of youthful curiosity for the first time in years.

"The leper was healed," her mother almost whispered.

Hannah raised her spindly fingers to her lips and gasped as if she had just discovered a hidden treasure. And as far as she was concerned, she had. Hannah kept saying to herself, "He touched a leper. I can't believe he touched a leper." The healing hadn't escaped her notice, but she was stunned by the willingness of this man to befriend the outcast, the unclean, and the forgotten, because that is what she had become.

Quickly, she gathered her things, along with a cloak to keep herself hidden from the crowds, and said to her mother and father, "I must go see Jesus. I just know that if I can see him and touch him, I will be healed." She ran through her doorway, waving to her parents, as if she were a child again. She now found herself in a sea of people baking in the hot sun and waiting for Jesus to come into Capernaum.

The minute Jesus appeared in the street, he was totally surrounded by the swarming crowd. Hannah caught just a glimpse of him before the crowd bumped her and pushed her away. She had no strength to fight through this throng of people to get to Jesus, but she knew that somehow she must! *Hannah,* she said sternly to herself, *you can do this.* Gathering every ounce of strength she could muster, she began to work her way through the crowd. She prayed that no one would recognize her, for if anyone did, she would be chased out of town.

Finally, out of breath and with little strength remaining, she found herself within a few feet of Jesus. She could see his smiling face through the sea of flailing arms. She came up behind him in the crowd and reached out to touch his cloak, thinking, *If I can just touch his clothes, I will be healed.* Straining, stretching, the tip of her fingers finally made contact with a fold of his cloak. Instantly, she felt a strangely refreshing sensation rush through her entire body, as if she had been drenched by a wave in the sea. Immediately her bleeding stopped, and she felt in her body that she was freed from her suffering.

In the same instant, Jesus realized that power had gone out from him. Whirling around, he asked, "Who touched my clothes?"

"You see the people crowding against you," his disciples answered, "and yet you ask, 'Who touched me?'" But Jesus kept looking around to see who had done it.

Then Hannah, knowing what had happened to her, came and fell at his feet and, trembling with fear, told him the whole truth. Jesus lifted Hannah to her feet and brushed away the tears that were pouring down her face. She hadn't felt the touch of a friend or anyone else in so long that her knees almost buckled from joy.

Jesus looked into her eyes, placed his arm around her, and gently said, "Daughter, your faith has healed you. Go in peace and be freed from your suffering."

As Jesus walked away, he kept his smiling eyes fastened on hers until he was interrupted by a group of men wanting to speak with him. Hannah framed those eyes in her mind and pledged never to forget them. The crowd moved past her and left her standing alone. Then Hannah turned and ran home to her parents and told them everything that had happened. She never went back to the little dwelling on the outskirts of town. She became the best friend of all those who were weak, helpless, and heartbroken.

Scriptural Account
MARK 5:24B-34

A large crowd followed and pressed around him. And a woman was there who had been subject to bleeding for twelve years. She had suffered a great deal under the care of many doctors and had spent all she had, yet instead of getting better she grew worse. When she heard about Jesus, she came up behind him in the crowd and touched his cloak, because she thought, "If I just touch his clothes, I will be healed." Immediately her bleeding stopped and she felt in her body that she was freed from her suffering.

At once Jesus realized that power had gone out from him. He turned around in the crowd and asked, "Who touched my clothes?"

"You see the people crowding against you," his disciples answered, "and yet you can ask, 'Who touched me?'"

But Jesus kept looking around to see who had done it. Then the woman, knowing what had happened to her, came and fell at his feet and, trembling with fear, told him the whole truth. He said to her, "Daughter, your faith has healed you. Go in peace and be freed from your suffering."

11

DEATH MEETS LIFE

Introduction

Have you ever wondered what it would be like to possess words that could bring healing to a sick person, sight to a blind man, strength to legs that have not walked in years, or even resurrect the dead? I have; and you probably have as well. It's not the adulation that drives the desire, nor the riches or the fame that it would bring. No, this hunger to be a healer comes strictly from a deep hatred for the enemies of life. Whether it is disease that threatens a life of good health or a mishap that has stolen one of the sacred gifts God has given, death is an enemy of life.

Imagine for a few minutes what it would be like to have the power of healing. You walk into a hospital room where the enemy, sickness, has laid claim to another victim. You notice the nail biting and head scratching as friends and family pray under their breath and look for answers. You walk over to the bed of fading life and touch the head of the sick person. You speak to the enemy with authority and drive it from the body, from the room, from the family, and from the earth. Victory shines as the light of hope over injustice.

You walk into a funeral home where loved ones have gathered to remember—not look forward to, or plan the future with—but to remember, because death has come and taken another victim. Tears and fears fill the room because of the deep sting of death. Like most enemies of life it doesn't honor youth, recognize love, or show respect for the righteous. But you, who possess the words of life that can destroy the enemy's work, walk to the cold casket where the enemy rests on his accomplishment, and you speak the words of life. The person is raised from death at your command. The celebration of life begins; it has faced death and death itself is no more. It feels good, doesn't it.

You may say, "But I don't have that power. I can't heal or resurrect the dead." If you believe that, the enemy has won already. You may not miraculously heal or resurrect the dead, but the fact is you meet the enemy every day in the streets where you live—on the job, where you meet with friends, and where you shop. He's right there behind the fake smiles and facades of people who are living in fear. But you possess the words of life that can heal broken spirits and resurrect dead hopes. The very words that came from the one who completely and utterly destroyed death are yours to speak and use in your life. They are powerful; don't sell them short. Speak the life-giving words of Christ. Say to the weak, "Do not let your hearts be troubled, trust in God"; to the lonely, "I will be with you always"; and to those who are discouraged and confused, "I have come so that they can have life and have it to the full."

Whatever you do, don't avoid confronting the enemy of life with the words of life. The end of the story will always say the same thing. The enemy is defeated and the victory is yours.

Death Meets Life

Abigail squinted in defense against the intruding morning light as she leaned against the doorpost of her modest home, and looked out on the empty street of her beloved village, Nain. Normally she loved early mornings, when her ritual led her to brush through her dark brown waves that covered her head until she tamed them and they lay quietly. Then she would kneel in prayer to her God before the sun arrived to announce the new day. After starting breakfast she would stand at her window until the sun revealed a glimpse of Mount Tabor to the northeast. The rounded peak invited her to dream of its peace and beauty when she wanted to escape her troubled thoughts. Then she would break away from the window and finish breakfast for herself and the son she so dearly loved, Daniel.

That was most mornings, but not this one. Today grief filled her home and her heart, much like her heavy frame and full dress filled every space of the doorway. She never conceived that she could feel as lost and lonely as she did right now. It wasn't that Abigail had not experienced darkness in her days. She had suffered the agony of loss more than once and could attest that there was nothing more damaging to the soul than losing those she loved.

Eight years earlier her parents and brother had perished together during a violent storm that blew in the walls of their home. She had just been betrothed to marry Jeremiah when it happened and she leaned heavily on him through the ordeal. He was her rock. He was a good man of noble character and great faith who loved to laugh and cherished his Abigail with all his heart. He was a builder and had constructed the home in which they lived with his own hands. He was highly skilled and in much demand. He had large round eyes, little hair, very dark skin from working in the sun all day, and a wide frame that was bulging with muscle. His greatest gift was not his talent of building, but that he knew what people needed and when they needed it. When Abigail's only living family was gone, he stepped in to love away the hurt and bring light and peace back to her eyes, and to give her their only child, Daniel.

Daniel was seven years old when the second meeting with death came, and this time it took the hero who had rescued her heart when she was most vulnerable. It stole her loving Jeremiah. He had died suddenly of a curious ailment that wracked his strong body and took him in two short days. She thought she would never again in this life feel the bitter loneliness and pain of those days leading to the burial and good byes she said to Jeremiah. Little did she know how that pain would be eclipsed by the events of the last few days. Even though Daniel was only seven when the tragedy took place he was his father's son and knew already that he would have to forgo his own pain and place his energy in bringing comfort to his mother. He told her that he would be the man around the house now. And that he was.

In many ways Daniel was all boy and all man at the same time. He was energetic, reckless, playful, sensitive, and he loved to laugh like his dad. He was also a town favorite like his dad had been, and he filled every crack and crevasse that was left in Abigail's heart by the loss of Jeremiah. On days that he sensed Abigail slipping into depression, he would gather her up and they would walk outside the city gates. They would look at the distant silhouette of Mount Tabor and talk about what it would be like to live at the very top, looking out on the world. Abigail would soon laugh with Daniel, and he would climb up one of the cypress trees that bordered the village and playfully beg her to join him. That was four years ago.

As Abigail now stood in that doorway and peered out at the once loved lavish tree Jeremiah had planted outside their home, she was surprised by how much she now despised it. She couldn't believe how her world had turned so dark so quickly. Daniel, in one of his playful moods, had climbed the tree with a friend and called for his mother to watch. She sprang from the door when she heard the crack of a branch that would not hold him. She watched in horror and covered a scream with her hand as she saw his head smash against the unforgiving earth below the tree. She ran and tried to gather him up but he was unconscious.

"No, no, no," she kept saying to herself as her neighbors lifted him and brought him into the house. She began to feel better as Daniel started regaining consciousness and smiled a faint smile up at her. But within a couple of hours she knew there was something desperately wrong. Daniel was throwing up and couldn't stay awake for more than a few minutes at a time. Once he awoke and looked at his mother's face and simply whimpered while saying "Momma, I don't know what's wrong" as he faded off again.

A physician came in to examine the boy, but he spoke only cold words. Neighbors prayed hard, and friends nervously waited with Abigail. The enemy, death, waited for his prey. By mid morning, Daniel stopped breathing and the cries of Abigail and all those who loved Daniel deeply could be heard all over Nain.

In the doorway this morning she asked questions of the air: "Has it really already been three days? Did it really happen so quickly? Have I really just lost everything I cared about?" The silent answer was a brutal, "Yes!" And the funeral for Daniel was to be today. She brushed aside another wave of tears that had streamed from her eyes so relentlessly that they threatened to make their own paths in her face. She sighed and spoke to heaven the question, "Why?" Heaven listened, and before the day was over she would meet heaven face to face. She would receive her answer.

In the silence she turned to enter the home that held no more joy for her. She could hardly bare the memories of Jeremiah, and now she couldn't even tolerate the thoughts of her only son whom she would never hold, kiss, laugh, or dream with again. She crumbled on the floor wanting to join them in death rather than face one more day without them. It seemed now there really was no reason to live. Death had won again. Wouldn't it always be victorious over mere mortals? *What a horrid enemy; what a sadistic foe,* she thought to herself. How can anyone face it and beat it back? It is a futile battle against an unbeatable adversary.

She lifted herself to prepare for the funeral procession that would lead to the burial field outside the city gates.

After an hour of preparation, Abigail stepped out her door and was met by a large, silent crowd from the city who loved her and loved Daniel. She walked through them whispering, "Thank you for coming." They came to walk with her to Daniel's last resting place, and tried to bring comfort and hope but knew they would accomplish nothing. No responses were given to her thanks. What could be said to a woman who just lost her only child and who was a widow with no living family. No words were worthy. They could only offer their presence to help fill the void as large as the heavens.

The procession began, slowly walking toward the city gates. Six men carried the body of Daniel in a coffin. With every step the wails became louder and the hopelessness became thicker. Suddenly there was another sound that filled the air. Not sounds of sorrow but of excited conversations and laughter. Abigail became quiet trying to find where the sound was originating. It was there, outside the city gates. Something or someone was coming with a large crowd, nearly as large as the one that surrounded her. They were coming toward her, just a few feet from where she now stood. As the funeral procession reached the gates of the city, the other crowd became visible. There was a man in front that was now intently staring at Abigail and the body being carried by the men. His eyes were gentle and his light smile instantly became an expression of compassion. Someone was heard saying, "Make way for the procession. This is a widow burying her only son." But Jesus already knew all about Abigail and her circumstances. As the two crowds crossed just outside the city gates Jesus had compassion on her, held up his hand for the crowd to stop, and said to Abigail, "Do not weep."

Surprisingly, she stopped weeping immediately and something deep within her told her that the procession of death had just encountered a procession of life. She couldn't explain it, but for the first time in three days peace swept across her heart. Both crowds were now completely still and not a word was uttered except by Jesus. He slowly walked to the coffin, touched the side, and said, "Young man, I say to you arise." Abigail found herself saying the word *arise*, over and over again in a whisper, as he who was dead sat up and began to speak. Jesus presented the hand of Abigail to the hand of Daniel, and with shrieks of joy she pulled Daniel from the coffin and began smothering him with kisses and hugs.

The crowds now mingled, and a moment of celebration overcame the whole group of people. There were no longer two crowds—one of death and one of life. They were now one great throng of one heart praising their God in awe and saying, "A great prophet has risen among us"; and "God has visited his people."

The report about what happened spread over all Judea and the surrounding area. No one told the story better than Abigail and Daniel. They would speak to anyone and everyone about the day they met Jesus. Daniel would tell of his accident and how his life was over. Abigail would talk of the funeral procession, and in perfect unison they would say: "Yes, that was the day that the enemy death met life." Then they would say in unison, "And death was the one that died."

Scriptural Account
LUKE 7:11-17

Soon afterward, Jesus went to a town called Nain, and his disciples and a large crowd went along with him. As he approached the town gate, a dead person was being carried out—the only son of his mother, and she was a widow. And a large crowd from the town was with her. When the Lord saw her, his heart went out to her and he said, "Don't cry."

Then he went up and touched the coffin, and those carrying it stood still. He said, "Young man, I say to you, get up!" The dead man sat up and began to talk, and Jesus gave him back to his mother.

They were all filled with awe and praised God. "A great prophet has appeared among us," they said. "God has come to help his people." This news about Jesus spread throughout Judea and the surrounding country.

12

An Unwanted Visitor and a Welcome Friend

Introduction

The attraction to Jesus was compelling. But what was it that made thousands want to be close to him? What was it that changed everyone who engaged the friendship of Jesus? We know that it wasn't his looks that attracted others. We are told that he was a common looking person. He might have looked like you or like me. In fact, he probably wanted us to see ourselves in him.

Certainly his appeal had something to do with the words he spoke. They were kind even to those who were not; they were forgiving to those who did not deserve it; and they were tender to the frailest of hearts.

And surely people were drawn to his inviting touch. His arms were always extended to the children, the heartbroken, the sick, and the mistreated. It's easy even now to see his busy hands warmly grasping the arms of new friends, placing the head of a weeping follower on his shoulder, or touching the cheek of a lost soul looking for life. And of course, one of the things that made friendship with Jesus so irresistible was his warm and wonderful promises: The promise of new life no matter how a person had misused the old one. The promise of never being hungry, thirsty, lost, or lonely. The promise that life is never over, even though it may seem so to the rest of the world.

Whatever it was that drew crowds to Christ, it changed forever those he befriended.

Even though you may never be followed by thousands of followers, you will have a great impact on your friends as you follow Christ. Simply let your words express love, your touch be inviting, and your promises always true. Even though your friendships may not be written down for history, those whom you befriend will say they were never the same after they called you friend.

An Unwanted Visitor and a Welcome Friend

The brilliance of the white sun on the Bethany landscape contrasted sharply with the mood of its citizenry. The normally bustling pace of its people had come to a startling halt. An unwelcome visitor had come to town. His cold shadow and frigid fingers had touched every individual within the town's borders. Even after he left, his hot breath served as a stinging reminder that he would return. The visitor was death.

In this instance, his numbing effect was intensified by his choice of victim. It seemed as though no one in this community, which served as the gateway to Jerusalem, was untouched by the deceased, Lazarus, or by his sisters, Mary and Martha. This beloved family had become well known as a friend to all in Bethany. Their concern for the hurting, hospitality to the hungry, kindness to the rejected, and benevolence to anyone who had need was legendary—not only in Bethany but all the way to Jerusalem.

Even four days after Lazarus was laid to rest in the tomb, many from Jerusalem remained in Bethany to comfort Martha and Mary in the loss of their brother. However, even in this time of great heartache, it was the sisters of Lazarus who did most of the comforting—and there were many to comfort, for everyone grieved the death of the man who had somehow become friend to so many. The man who had become a fixture of fondness with his busy and affectionate hands, tall frame, long gait, and perpetually bright smile was gone. The pain of loss could be measured in the longing eyes, expressionless faces, silenced tongues, and tear-stained cheeks of those in Bethany.

There had been a time, however, when Bethany would not have mourned the death of Lazarus or bothered to mourn with his sisters. Indeed, the community might have even quietly cheered the demise of the likes of Lazarus. For in the not-too-distant past, the reputation of Lazarus and his sisters was the subject of venomous gossip on the street corners and cruel whispers at the market. Lazarus had been described by most who knew him as distant, self-serving, prideful, and mean. The townspeople knew to keep their distance when Lazarus walked down the street. Mary was infamous for her rebellious spirit and brutally honest tongue. Martha was regarded as a hermit who rarely appeared in public, and when she did, she said nothing to anyone. Many speculated that she had an evil spirit or was a mental cripple.

But on a visit to Jerusalem for a religious feast, something remarkable had happened. On the last day of the Feast of Tabernacles, Lazarus and Martha were standing in the temple courts when they heard a man speaking. He was saying things the two of them had never heard before, and his words cracked the brittle shell that had formed around their hearts. Lazarus and Martha asked those around them who the man was. They said his name was Jesus. Some of them whispered that he was a prophet; others said he was evil. Lazarus and Martha just wanted to hear more.

Finally, Jesus stood up and said, "If a man is thirsty, let him come to me and drink. Whoever believes in me, as the

Scripture has said, streams of water will flow from within him." This caused quite a stir in the crowd, but it caused a raging storm of emotion in Lazarus and Martha. They came to Jesus and said, "We are thirsty; we want to hear more, teacher." Jesus answered, "Then you shall, my friends, come follow me."

The next day Jesus appeared again in the temple court, and a crowd gathered, including Lazarus, Martha, and now Mary. As he was teaching, a half-naked woman was hurled down at his feet. A group of religious leaders had set her up with the husband of a woman in town so they could catch her and test Jesus on how he would judge her. Mary's eyes flashed with anger as they told Jesus they had caught her in the act of adultery and that Moses would have her put to death.

Fear gripped Mary, Lazarus, and Martha as the group of men began to pick up stones to throw at the woman. But Jesus bent down next to the accused, looked at her with an assuring expression, and began to write something on the ground. When he straightened, he said to the accusers; "If any one of you is without sin, let him begin stoning her."

Martha closed her eyes, expecting the worst. Then she began to hear the dull thud of stones dropping harmlessly to the ground. The accusers walked away, and Jesus stood alone with the prostitute. Mary didn't hear the entire exchange, but she did hear him say, "Then neither do I condemn you, go now and leave your life of sin."

As the woman walked away, a stunned Mary felt a softening in her own heart and was drawn to the overwhelming mercy of this unusual man who dared challenge the false justice of these hypocritical men.

After spending a few more days with Jesus, Lazarus, Martha, and Mary returned to Bethany with beaming smiles, sparkling eyes, and transformed hearts. Everyone wanted to know what had brought such a stunning change. Over and over again, they told the story of their new friendship with a man who had touched them as no one ever had. As they told the story, the three offered the kind of friendship they had found in Jesus, and the love for Lazarus, Mary, and Martha blossomed throughout Bethany.

Then within the last couple of weeks, neighbors began to notice a slowing in Lazarus's gait. His color turned pale, his breathing became labored, and though he never stopped smiling, pain seeped into his expression from time to time. He had collapsed a week ago and had told Mary and Martha he felt the life draining from him. Word was sent to Jesus. Surely he would want to come and heal his friend the way he had healed so many others. But he tarried, and when he finally arrived, it was too late. The unwelcome visitor had arrived first, and his visit left an occupied tomb and empty hearts.

Suddenly a stir began among the crowd. Jesus had arrived. Martha had gone out to meet him, and then he sent for Mary. Mary fell at Jesus' feet, saying, "Lord, if you had been here, my brother would not have died."

When Jesus saw her weeping, along with all those who had come out with her, he was deeply moved and troubled. And then Jesus wept. At this display of emotion, several in the crowd remarked how much Jesus must have loved Lazarus.

Jesus, deeply moved, came to the tomb with an expression that had changed from sorrow to confrontation, and he spoke firmly, saying, "Take away the stone." Martha reminded Jesus that by this time the body would smell. Jesus placed his hands on her shoulders and said, "Did I not tell you that if you believed, you would see the glory of God?" After lifting his eyes toward heaven and saying a short prayer, Jesus faced the tomb. With a thundering voice, he exclaimed, "Lazarus, come out!"

Inside the tomb, eyes were opened, a heart resumed its rhythmic beat, and the strength of life filled a dead body. When Lazarus appeared at the mouth of the tomb, a stunned crowd watched in utter silence. Jesus smiled at Lazarus and said, "Take off the grave clothes and let him go." Mary and Martha, along with several others, rushed to Lazarus, tore the wrappings from him, and smothered him with embracing arms.

The hands that had been covered in the cloth of the dead became active and affectionate once again. The legs and feet that were wrapped for burial resumed their welcomed, long strides. A face once covered for the sleep of death now beamed a bright smile, reflecting the heart of a town whose best friend had just returned.

Above all, the power of friendship in the visitor named Jesus proved greater than the power of the destruction in the unwelcome visit of death.

Scriptural Account

JOHN 8:3-11; 11:1-3, 17-29, 32-44

The teachers of the law and the Pharisees brought in a woman caught in adultery. They made her stand before the group and said to Jesus, "Teacher, this woman was caught in the act of adultery. In the Law Moses commanded us to stone such women. Now what do you say?" They were using this question as a trap, in order to have a basis for accusing him.

But Jesus bent down and started to write on the ground with his finger. When they kept on questioning him, he straightened up and said to them, "If any one of you is without sin, let him be the first to throw a stone at her." Again he stooped down and wrote on the ground.

At this, those who heard began to go away one at a time, the older ones first, until only Jesus was left, with the woman still standing there. Jesus straightened up and asked her, "Woman, where are they? Has no one condemned you?"

"No one, sir," she said.

"Then neither do I condemn you," Jesus declared. "Go now and leave your life of sin."

Now a man named Lazarus was sick. He was from Bethany, the village of Mary and her sister Martha. This Mary, whose brother Lazarus now lay sick, was the same one who poured perfume on

the Lord and wiped his feet with her hair. So the sisters sent word to Jesus, "Lord, the one you love is sick."

On his arrival, Jesus found that Lazarus had already been in the tomb for four days. Bethany was less than two miles from Jerusalem, and many Jews had come to Martha and Mary to comfort them in the loss of their brother. When Martha heard that Jesus was coming, she went out to meet him, but Mary stayed at home.

"Lord," Martha said to Jesus, "if you had been here, my brother would not have died. But I know that even now God will give you whatever you ask."

Jesus said to her, "Your brother will rise again."

Martha answered, "I know he will rise again in the resurrection at the last day."

Jesus said to her, "I am the resurrection and the life. He who believes in me will live, even though he dies; and whoever lives and believes in me will never die. Do you believe this?"

"Yes, Lord," she told him, "I believe that you are the Christ, the Son of God, who was to come into the world."

And after she had said this, she went back and called her sister Mary aside. "The Teacher is here," she said, "and is asking for you." When Mary heard this, she got up quickly and went to him.

When Mary reached the place where Jesus was and saw him, she fell at his feet and said, "Lord, if you had been here, my brother would not have died."

When Jesus saw her weeping, and the Jews who had come along with her also weeping, he was deeply moved in spirit and troubled. "Where have you laid him?" he asked.

"Come and see, Lord," they replied.

Jesus wept.

Then the Jews said, "See how he loved him!"

But some of them said, "Could not he who opened the eyes of the blind man have kept this man from dying?"

Jesus, once more deeply moved, came to the tomb. It was a cave with a stone laid across the entrance. "Take away the stone," he said.

"But, Lord," said Martha, the sister of the dead man, "by this time there is a bad odor, for he has been there four days."

Then Jesus said, "Did I not tell you that if you believed, you would see the glory of God?"

So they took away the stone. Then Jesus looked up and said, "Father, I thank you that you have heard me. I knew that you always hear me, but I said this for the benefit of the people standing here, that they may believe that you sent me."

When he had said this, Jesus called in a loud voice, "Lazarus, come out!" The dead man came out, his hands and feet wrapped with strips of linen, and a cloth around his face.

Jesus said to them, "Take off the grave clothes and let him go."

SECTION FOUR

GIFTS

13

THE EXTRAVAGANT GIFT

Introduction

If you were asked to describe friendship, what would you say? You might use words like loyalty, faithfulness, dedication, and devotion. You might think of the characteristics of friendship, like sensitivity, sharing, understanding, or gentleness.

However, there is another way to describe friendship that reflects its beauty and blessings in perhaps a more adequate way. It may not be something that would simply pop into your mind, but if you think about it, you will probably agree. A proper description of friendship is "an extravagant gift." If you look up the word extravagant in the dictionary, you will find in its definition the phrase, "exceeding the bounds of reason." The word *gift* is defined as something given without any repayment expected. Now isn't that a perfect way to describe good friendship?

Examine the extravagant gifts of true friendship. Time is offered without counting seconds or minutes. When friends are called, they come without glancing at their watches or wondering when they will no longer be needed. Resources are offered without restriction. When friends are in need, there are no whys, whats, wheres, or whens exchanged. There is simply the sound of an opening wallet or heart. When friends hurt, compassion is felt and comfort offered. One cannot weep without the other tasting salt and wiping away tears.

And what about the gifts exchanged? A friend will search with reckless abandon until the perfect present is found, fitted, or formed. In other words, self is sacrificed for the sake of someone else.

You have a friend who fits this description perfectly. He gave you the extravagant gift of his life. He saw the nails being placed in his hands and feet before it ever happened, and he never turned away. His friendship with you wouldn't let him. He saw you as an extravagant gift worth having. He also knew that you would be a true friend to others.

The Extravagant Gift

Mary brushed her thick, black, waist-length hair away from her face in an effort to persuade it not to distract her from her work. As her slender, well-worked fingers masterfully kneaded the dough that would soon become a tasty companion to an already delightful meal, she periodically wiped her hands across the heavily stained apron that wrapped around her thin waist. Her dark eyes—perched on her high, well-defined cheekbones—danced with excitement. She could hardly contain the elation she felt as the evening celebration drew nearer. She looked over at her sister, Martha, and smiled broadly as she said, "Won't it be wonderful to have so many of our friends with us tonight?" And with added emphasis she exclaimed, "Especially our honored guest, Jesus!"

The older, much heavier, and much more serious Martha returned an uneasy smile and said, "Yes, I just hope we have enough food for everyone."

Mary looked at what she felt was a rather excessive mound of food and raised her hand to her mouth to keep from laughing out loud at her sister's needless concern. "Martha," Mary chuckled, "we have enough food here to serve the whole Roman army."

Martha ran the back of her hand against the sides of her head, making sure that her hair was neatly pulled back and no rebellious strands of gray had escaped. She then sighed a sigh Mary had become all too familiar with and said, "It may look like enough to you, but when everyone arrives, it will go very quickly. You know how those fishermen eat. Why, Peter and his brother almost eat their weight in food every time they sit down to a meal. I just want everything to be perfect."

Mary reached out and reassuringly stroked Martha on the back and said the words she had repeated a hundred times before, whenever Martha showed undue concern: "Dear sister, you are the greatest hostess the world has ever known. Your meals are near perfection, and there is always food to spare. Why, if I were going to invite a king to our home, I wouldn't think of asking anyone but you to handle the whole affair."

Even though Martha answered Mary's statement of confidence with a self-deprecating, "Well, I don't know about that," she always appreciated hearing Mary's encouraging words because she knew she really did mean them. Martha, it seemed, was always in need of reassurance, and the perceptive Mary was delighted to provide it.

While Mary waited for the dough to rise, she moved to the doorway that opened to the road running through the middle of Bethany. As she looked toward the east, she could see the swirling clouds of dust in the distance being raised by the mounting crowds headed toward Jerusalem. She imagined the countless sandaled feet, rolling wagon wheels, and animal hooves that were stirring the earth on the way to the Passover. She could practically hear the clutter of conversation between friends and family about everything from politics and power to parenting and marriage. The throngs of worshipers were still a day away from converging on Mary's beloved Bethany, the town that served as the gateway to the Mount of Olives and Jerusalem. Mary herself would soon be among them, covering the day's walk to the holy city to celebrate the most wonderful of all holidays—the day when God spared his people with the blood of the lamb.

Turning her gaze to the west, Mary looked toward the peak of the hill that looked out over the holy city on the other side. In the distance she recognized the familiar silhouette of Jesus walking with his disciples toward Bethany. He was wiping the moisture from his forehead and speaking passionately to his disciples. Mary called out to Martha, "They're coming! Martha, they're coming down the road right now."

Mary heard Martha's muted voice as she passed by the window saying something about getting the bread baked, but Mary was already running toward the group of welcome friends. As she came closer to the group, Mary could tell by

Jesus' expression that he was telling his friends something of great importance. Jesus' moist eyes met Mary's at the exact time she heard him say, "As you know, the Passover is just days away, and the Son of Man will be handed over to be crucified."

The words hit her hard, making her feel as though someone had pushed her back on her heels. Some of those with Jesus shook their heads and whispered, "What is he saying; they won't try to hurt him." She heard Peter declare, "Just let them try; we'll protect him!" Jesus didn't move his eyes an inch; he just looked into Mary's eyes and nodded in a way that told her it would happen just as he said.

Mary felt herself almost stop breathing as she heard the first clap of thunder and looked behind Jesus at the storm clouds gathering over Jerusalem. Suddenly Jesus' teachings came rushing through her mind like a flash flood, and she remembered the words *Passover, Lamb of God, the blood of the Lamb, God spared his people.* Jesus was now standing before her, and he gathered her in his arms and embraced her; and with a whisper in her ear, he said, "You understand, don't you, Mary?"

Lazarus, whom Jesus had raised from the dead, came running up to the group from the house exclaiming for all to hear, "Come everyone, a dinner has been prepared in honor of Jesus. Martha has everything prepared; it is a feast you will certainly not forget."

With that, the disciples followed behind Lazarus to the house while Mary walked alongside Jesus in shocked silence. As they reached the door, the others went in and reclined. But Mary stopped Jesus and with tears now flowing from her eyes, she asked, "Is there no other way?"

Jesus said nothing; he simply wiped the tears from Mary's cheek and joined his friends. Mary stood at the door a moment longer, looking up the road and examining the gathering storm. She then walked into the house and past the perturbed Martha, who was now serving their friends the meal.

Mary didn't even hear Martha as she chided her to help with the food. She went to the next room and directly to a large chest in the corner. She lifted the heavy lid and began looking for something hidden deep inside. When her hands grasped what she was looking for, a fiat smile appeared on her face. As she lifted her hand, a beautiful alabaster jar appeared. She knelt down and lifted the jar and her voice toward heaven, "My God, you are my God, and the One you have sent is the Lamb. He is also my teacher, my hope, my strength, and my closest friend. This alabaster jar of perfume neither costs enough nor smells beautiful enough for what it is about to be used. It was intended for my wedding night, but now I use it to prepare a loved one for burial—the One you have sent. My heart breaks like this jar, but my soul is filled with the fragrance of hope."

Mary entered the room that was now filled with bustling conversation and laughter. She stood behind the silent Jesus, broke open the jar, and poured the pint of pure nard on his head. As the perfume moved down his hair and onto his shoulders, Jesus closed his eyes and breathed deeply so that the perfume filled his nostrils and lungs. Mary took some of the perfume and poured it on his feet. Knowing this would be one of the last times she would have him with her, she ached for the holy moment to linger, like the aroma that now filled every space of the small home. To keep the anointing alive in her heart for as long as she could, she took her hair from around her back, pulled it over her shoulders, and held the thick strands in her hand. She then began to gently wipe his feet with her hair so that his fragrance would remain on her, with her, and in her memories for as long as she lived.

The room went quiet until the silence was broken by Judas, who said, "Why wasn't this perfume sold and the money given to the poor? It was worth a year's wages."

"Leave her alone," Jesus replied. "It was meant that she should save this perfume for the day of my burial." As Mary arose, Jesus said, "You will always have the poor among you, but you will not always have me." As Mary started to move away, Jesus arose and gave her another embrace and whispered to her once more, "This extravagant gift of friendship will never be forgotten."

Mary looked into his eyes and whispered back to him, "Neither will the extravagant gift you are about to give."

Mary walked slowly toward the door, holding her hair close to her face. Standing outside, she watched the growing storm clouds gather over Jerusalem.

Scriptural Account

JOHN 12:1-8

Six days before the Passover, Jesus arrived at Bethany, where Lazarus lived, whom Jesus had raised from the dead. Here a dinner was given in Jesus' honor. Martha served, while Lazarus was among those reclining at the table with him. Then Mary took about a pint of pure nard, an expensive perfume; she poured it on Jesus' feet and wiped his feet with her hair. And the house was filled with the fragrance of the perfume.

But one of his disciples, Judas Iscariot, who was later to betray him objected, "Why wasn't this perfume sold and the money given to the poor? It was worth a year's wages." He did not say this because he cared for the poor but because he was a thief; as keeper of the money bag, he used to help himself to what was put into it.

"Leave her alone," Jesus replied, "It was intended that she should save this perfume for the day of my burial. You will always have the poor among you, but you will not always have me."

14

FORGIVENESS

Introduction

Friends share a special something that is rich, rare, powerful, and persuasive. They offer it without cost to each other and yet it
holds extreme value. If it were a commodity, it would be considered
priceless. If it were a precious stone, its value would be immeasur-
able. If it were a painting, it would be the most coveted of all works
of art. What is it? *Forgiveness*—one simple word, phrase, or touch
that transforms heartbreak into healing, sadness into celebration,
and tragedy into triumph.

Forgiveness from a friend brings restoration and renewal that
sends the heart soaring. Forgiveness changes the direction of a

friend's path, alters the plans for the future, and changes the darkness of night into the light of morning. Don't ever doubt the power of forgiveness, and never believe the lie that friends never let each other down. In fact, friendship may be measured by the weight of the forgiveness granted or received.

Close your eyes, and let the shadow of a cross two thousand years old move across your heart and define friendship and forgiveness. Feel its weight as it is lifted off of your shoulders and placed on One who calls you friend. That friend took your nails, your thorns, your spear, and your transgressions and offered you his forgiveness. He did it to show that failures are not fatal and that the soil of friendship raises a harvest of forgiveness.

You may be the friend who needs forgiveness, or you may be the one granting it. You may be the friend who needs to offer it, or the one who needs to ask for it. Either way, go ahead and do what the supreme friendship calls you to do with this assurance in your heart: once forgiveness is given or accepted, no power on earth can dilute the love and loyalty it produces.

Forgiveness

As he raised his face toward heaven, he breathed deeply through his long, narrow, sun-baked nose, trying to catch every bit of the salty sea wind blowing over him from the southeast. He had forgotten the strangely alluring fragrance during his past three years of travel. Although the once familiar smells emanating from the Sea of Galilee should have brought the welcomed comfort of returning home to this northwest shore community, for Peter the disciple, it had the completely opposite effect. The sandy beach he had once fished from for his livelihood held no appeal for him now.

Peter had left this place of his youth and young adulthood three years ago on a mission, and coming back here meant a retreat from that mission—and Peter wasn't the sort who liked to retreat from anything. As he looked wistfully along the shoreline, Peter's thoughts drifted through those three eventful years.

He thought first of that fateful day when, just a few short steps from where he now sat, Jesus had voiced the simple words that would change his path, passion, and purpose. Peter mouthed the words and whispered them faintly to himself: "Come, follow me," Jesus had said, "and I will make you fishers of men." As the words echoed through his mind, the mixture of the salt air and the voice that hung on the wind on that life-changing day stung his weary heart with sadness and wrung tears from his dark eyes. It had seemed so easy to drop everything and follow this average man with the extraordinary magnetism.

He then turned his gaze out to the sea and squinted as if to pinpoint the place where, at the invitation of his teacher, leader, and most trusted friend, he had actually walked on top of the water. Peter closed his eyes and wiggled his toes as he tried to recapture the astounding sensation of feeling the waves become solid under every step. But his smile quickly gave way to a frown as Peter remembered the embarrassment of falling under the waves after becoming frightened by the wind. He looked longingly at the wrist Jesus had so firmly grasped to rescue him from the angry sea. Peter now whispered, as if speaking to someone close by, "You were always rescuing me from something weren't you?"

With the words still fresh on his lips, the one memory Peter wanted to forget more than any other rushed into his heart like an unexpected squall. Suddenly Peter imagined himself in a courtyard. Curious onlookers asked him if he was one of the disciples of this Jesus who had just been turned over to the authorities for trial. As he watched the scene unfold in his mind, he heard himself say, "I don't know what you're talking about."

Again he heard the question, and again he heard himself say those horrible words: "I don't know the man." Peter tried to stop the nightmarish scene that ran through his mind, but he couldn't. The final denial came bursting through all his defenses, and he heard the words loud and clear, emphasized with a curse, "I don't know the man!"

The courtyard scene went dramatically silent as he recalled the crowing of a rooster and the lone figure of Jesus standing among his tormentors. Jesus' eyes had locked on to Peter's, and tears had run down Jesus' bloodied cheeks.

Peter now stood and looked painfully toward the heavens. Angrily, he beat his chest and shouted toward the now darkening sky, "Why did I forsake you? You were always rescuing me from something, and I couldn't even stand with you in your time of greatest need." And he fell to the sand and wept as bitterly as he had the night of the denial.

Now, when Peter's friends, Thomas, Nathaniel, James, and John—who were with him on the beach—saw Peter fall to the ground and openly weep, they rushed to see what was wrong. Peter looked up into their concerned faces, stood and hugged each one, and simply said, "I'm going out to fish." In unison, they all replied, "We'll go with you."

Early the next morning, after a frustrating and fruitless night of fishing, a lone figure stood on the beach and called out to them, "Friends," he said, "haven't you caught any fish?"

"No," they answered disgustedly.

The mysterious figure called out again, "Throw your net on the right side of the boat, and you will find some."

When they did, their net became so full of fish that they were unable to haul it in.

John was the first to recognize the man on the shore and said almost in a whisper, "It is the Lord!" Peter squinted his eyes to see if he could verify the words of John, then jumped into the water and swam for shore, riding each wave as far as he could, while the others towed the net full of fish.

When Peter reached the shore, he stopped short of where Jesus stood and looked longingly at him while panting heavily. Nothing was said between them until Jesus took his outer cloak and wrapped it around Peter, pointed at a fire of burning coals where fish were cooking, and said to all of them, "Bring some of the fish you have caught."

None of them dared ask who he was for in their hearts they knew it was the Lord. When they had finished eating Jesus moved behind Peter, placed his hands on his shoulders, and said, "Simon son of John, do you truly love me more than these?"

Peter looked at the others one by one then looked down to the sand and softly said, "Yes, Lord, you know that I love you."

Jesus replied, "Feed my lambs."

Jesus now moved to the right of Peter and knelt down beside him with his hand on his right shoulder and again said, "Simon son of John, do you truly love me?"

Peter, not wanting to meet the eyes of Jesus, looked off toward the sea and spoke more firmly, "Yes Lord, you know that I love you."

While rubbing Peters shoulders, Jesus replied once more, "Take care of my sheep."

Jesus now moved and sat directly in front of Peter, put both hands on his shoulders, looked into Peter's eyes, and slowly and deliberately asked for the third time, "Simon son of John, do you love me?"

Peter, feeling hurt because Jesus asked him the third time, placed his own hands on the shoulders of Jesus, and with tears running from his eyes into his beard said slowly and deliberately, "Lord, you know all things; you know that I love you."

With the three haunting denials of Jesus answered by the three affirmations of Peter's love, Jesus lifted Peter to his feet and said, "Feed my sheep." As Jesus spoke of the future with Peter, he took Peter's hand and led him a few steps from where they were standing. Once more, Jesus placed his hands on the shoulders of Peter and said, "Follow me!" After embracing Jesus, Peter realized that Jesus had led him to the exact place on the beach where three years earlier he had heard that same voice say those same words. Now assured of his friend's forgiveness, Peter whispered to himself, "Anywhere."

Scriptural Account

JOHN 21:3-13, 15-19

"I'm going out to fish," Simon Peter told them, and they said, *"We'll go with you."* So they went out and got into the boat, but that night they caught nothing.

Early in the morning, Jesus stood on the shore, but the disciples did not realize that it was Jesus.

He called out to them, *"Friends, haven't you any fish?"*

"No," they answered.

He said, *"Throw your net on the right side of the boat and you will find some."* When they did they were unable to haul the net in because of the large number of fish.

Then the disciple whom Jesus loved said to Peter, *"It is the Lord!"* As soon as Simon Peter heard him say, *"It is the Lord,"* he wrapped his outer garment around him (for he had taken it off) and jumped into the water. The other disciples followed in the boat, towing the net full of fish, for they were not far from shore, about a hundred yards. When they landed, they saw a fire of burning coals there with fish on it, and some bread.

Jesus said to them, *"Bring some of the fish you have just caught."*

Simon Peter climbed aboard and dragged the net ashore. It was full of large fish, 153, but even with so many the net was not torn. Jesus said to them, *"Come and have breakfast."* None of the disciples dared ask him, *"Who are you?"* They knew it was the

Lord. Jesus came, took the bread and gave it to them, and did the same with the fish.

❧

When they had finished eating, Jesus said to Simon Peter, "Simon son of John, do you truly love me more than these?"

"Yes, Lord," he said, "you know that I love you."

Jesus said, "Feed my lambs."

Again Jesus said, "Simon son of John, do you truly love me?"

He answered, "Yes, Lord, you know that I love you."

Jesus said, "Take care of my sheep."

The third time he said to him, "Simon son of John, do you love me?"

Peter was hurt because Jesus asked him the third time. "Do you love me?" He said, "Lord, you know all things; you know that I love you."

Jesus said, "Feed my sheep. I tell you the truth, when you were younger you dressed yourself and went where you wanted; but when you are old you will stretch out your hands, and someone else will dress you and lead you where you do not want to go." Jesus said this to indicate the kind of death by which Peter would glorify God. Then he said to him, "Follow me!"

15

NEVER FORGET
THE WAY BACK

Introduction

There is an old saying that has been used so frequently that you might easily miss its meaning—but don't. The saying goes like this: "A friend in need is a friend indeed." Whoever coined that phrase spoke volumes about friendship in eight short words.

Where do you turn when you feel crushed by concerns, weary from work, lonely from loss, or stricken by sickness? Who do you picture when you need to see a light at the end of the tunnel, hope at the end of a long road of struggle, or need to feel comfort after enduring a long stretch of sadness? Who comes to mind when you long for understanding and acceptance after you have failed both yourself and others? Who makes you laugh when you feel like weeping, or warms your heart when you feel as though you're in a deep freeze? More than likely you would say the name of a person who lives the very words of the saying, "A friend in need is a friend indeed."

Even though you might not know it, your face would be pictured by others who consider you a friend. Friendship brings a rush of responsibility to care, to act, to move, to comfort, to encourage, and to restore. Friends offer out-stretched arms to console, a kind touch to soothe, a shoulder to lean on, and an ear to hear.

The best friend the world has ever known said it best, "Come to me, all you who are weary and burdened, and I will give you rest." Isn't that a true friend? A person who allows you to escape the sadness, struggles, flaws, and failures and simply encourages you to rest.

The world needs friends like you, so keep your arms, eyes, and ears wide open. When you need a friend, don't hesitate to call on one. When you see someone who needs you, don't hesitate to offer the words "Come to me."

Never Forget the Way Back

"Only a little farther," Josiah said to himself, panting with each labored step. "Only a little farther, and I'll be home." To anyone else, the words and thoughts of home would have brought comfort—but not to Josiah. The thought of home was cloaked with apprehension and shame. He wiped his weathered brow with the filthy sleeve of his outer garment, and for the first time in days, he began to think about his ragged appearance. Feet that had at one time worn the finest footwear were now bare, bleeding, and caked with dirt and mud. He had traded his fine shoes for some measly morsels of bread a few days before. A body that had once been clothed in the finest of silks and woven wool was now covered in apparel made of tattered burlap, fashioned from sacks that had once contained feed for pigs. The elegant clothing had been surrendered to pay off gambling debts months ago. But the greatest embarrassment of all was his hands. Fingers that had been adorned with priceless gold and stones were naked, swollen, scarred, and calloused.

It was the first finger of his right hand that caused the most excruciating pain and forced Josiah to his knees, weeping and rocking back and forth while tremors of remorse swept though him. This was the finger that had worn the ring that bore his family seal. It was pure gold, and on the flat surface that surrounded a glistening diamond were the words *Faithfulness and Mercy*. It was now gone, stolen by one of the many "friends" who had disappeared when his money ran out.

Josiah remembered well the day his father, Emmanuel, gave it to him. It was two years ago, on the day before Josiah left home to begin a new life. He was full of hope, dreams, and more money than sense, supplied by his inheritance. Emmanuel, during a going-away party, had placed the ring on Josiah's finger and, with a prayer of blessing, said, "Almighty God, as I place this ring on Josiah's finger, I ask you to hold him close to your breast, bless him, and protect him. He is my son, my friend, my right hand, my joy and crown. Never, ever let him forget that true love and friendship will always be found at home." The words had made him burn with anger at the time. Now, they were like flames that licked at his heart and scorched him with sorrow and regret.

Josiah couldn't even remember exactly what had motivated him to leave his father and his brother Joseph. He did recall some big plans that he and his three friends had discussed when they left for the Decapolis, a city that had grown from ten different communities into one bustling metropolis. But every memory of the preceding two years seemed to blur in an accelerating downward spiral, until a few days ago. That's the day Josiah awoke.

First, his eyes were awakened by the screeching cries from a herd of pigs, among which he was now sleeping. Then, his heart was awakened by a cold realization: he was hungry, and not just for food, but for warmth, acceptance, love, and true friendship. He also realized for the first time that he was dying in every conceivable way a person can die. He was perishing physically, emotionally, and spiritually.

It was there amid the pigs, filth, loneliness, sorrow, and shame that Josiah remembered home and the words his father had prayed: "Never let him forget that true love and friendship will always be found at home." When he came to his senses, he said, "How many of my father's hired men have food to spare, and here I am starving to death! I will set out and go back to my father and say to him, 'Father, I have sinned against heaven and against you. I am no longer worthy to be called your son; make me like one of your hired men.'"

Now as he raised his eyes, he saw his home. It sat up on a hill, and under the blazing orange of the setting sun, it glistened like a jewel rising above the golden landscape. Memories flooded his soul. There on that hill to the right of the house, he, Emmanuel, and Joseph had lain together one afternoon, peering up into the sky and describing the different shapes the clouds formed. The huge olive tree to the left was where Emmanuel had taught the brothers to climb and persevere, explaining to them that the view from the top was worth the effort of the climb. Josiah now wondered how he could ever have left such a place, and he said to himself, "Dad, you were right; this is where true love and friendship are found." His pace quickened, and he practiced again what he would say when he faced his father, placing emphasis on the words that expressed his remorse and repentance.

The road crossed a stream where he stopped for a much needed drink and to wash away the dust from his journey and refresh himself for the coming moments.

As he lowered his head over the water, he saw his reflection for the first time in ages. The face that stared back at him was hideously gaunt and drawn. All signs of youth were gone, replaced by sharp cheekbones, sagging eyes, and harshly weathered skin. In disgust he slapped at the water as if to erase the reflection. All of the anticipation he had felt drained from him in an instant. He arose, looked at his home one more time, and said, "I will not shame you any more than I have." He then turned to walk away.

Suddenly, faintly, he heard his name, "Josiah, Josiah!" The voice became louder with every repetition. Josiah turned to see his father with his robe pulled up above his knees, running at full gallop.

Josiah stood motionless, wanting so much to run to Emmanuel but still full of apprehension. Tears poured from his eyes as he realized that his father was both laughing and crying while saying the words, "You're home, Josiah; you're home!" Before Josiah could say anything, Emmanuel threw his arms around him, almost knocking both of them to the ground. Emmanuel kissed Josiah repeatedly, and between each kiss he said, "Josiah, Josiah, you're home!"

Josiah tried to hold him at arm's length so that he could say the words that he had practiced so diligently, "Father, I have sinned against heaven and against you. I am no longer worthy to be called your son."

But Emmanuel smiled and shook his head at Josiah's words. "Do you still not understand, my son?" He then called for his servants, "Quick! Bring the best robe and put it on him, and get some sandals for his feet." Then Emmanuel took his own signet ring, placed it on the first finger of Josiah's right hand, and said, "True love and friendship will always be found at home."

With that, Emmanuel said, "Bring the fattened calf and kill it. Let's have a feast and celebrate. For this son of mine was dead and is alive again; he was lost and is found." So they began to celebrate the son's return with joy.

Scriptural Account

LUKE 15: 11-24

There was a man who had two sons. The younger one said to his father, "Father, give me my share of the estate." So he divided his property between them.

Not long after that, the younger son got together all he had, set off for a distant county and there squandered his wealth in wild living. After he had spent everything, there was a severe famine in that whole county, and he began to be in need. So he went and hired himself out to a citizen of that country, who sent him to his fields to feed pigs. He longed to fill his stomach with the pods that the pigs were eating, but no one gave him anything.

When he came to his senses, he said, "How many of my father's hired men have food to spare, and here I am starving to death! I will set out and go back to my father and say to him; Father, I have sinned against heaven and against you. I am no longer worthy to be called your son; make me like one of your hired men." So he got up and went to his father.

But while he was still a long way off, his father saw him and was filled with compassion for him; he ran to his son, threw his arms around him and kissed him.

The son said to him, "Father, I have sinned against heaven and against you. I am no longer worthy to be called your son."

But the father said to his servants, "Quick! Bring the best robe and put it on him. Put a ring on his finger and sandals on his feet.

Bring the fattened calf and kill it. Let's have a feast and celebrate. For this son of mine was dead and is alive again; he was lost and is found." So they began to celebrate.

SECTION FIVE

RECEIVE

16

MESSENGERS OF COURAGE

Introduction

Are you tired of running the race of life? Are you carrying more weight on your shoulders than you can safely handle? Are you consumed by a quiet desperation when you think about the future? Do you crave a simpler, more balanced life?

I have some good news for you. My message is not profound, but it will bring a light to your eyes and courage to your heart. Are you ready? You have a Father who loves you deeply. And he is waiting for you at home—your real home, in heaven.

Pretty simple, isn't it? God's Word tells us that thoughts of God's love and home helped Jesus endure the Cross. During his last and most stressful week on earth, he spoke of his Father's house and the many rooms being prepared for you.

Can you picture it? The fresh fragrance of new construction fills the place. The air holds excitement and anticipation. The warm love of the Living God illuminates each room and every hallway. No fear lurks in the darkness because there is no darkness there. And listen, do you hear the music? It's the joyful song of the angels. You can't help but join the chorus.

Approach the doorway where Jesus stands. With one nail-scarred hand he points to a golden nameplate that bears your name. Hear his gentle voice say, "One day you will be with me in this place, and all that you are going through now will seem as nothing."

Until that day, don't take your eyes off the love of the Father or the place he has prepared for you. Everything else will pass, but your home will stand forever.

Messengers of Courage

They entered the Garden of Gethsemane as darkness chased away dusk's lingering light. Jesus looked at the horizon as the last ember of sunlight disappeared at the fine line that separates earth and sky. His disciples followed close behind, sensing the mysterious sorrow behind the eyes of the magnificent man they had followed these three years. At supper they had listened to Jesus speak of strange, final things, and now they exchanged quizzical glances, hoping that perhaps one of them had an answer to what it all meant.

John quietly asked, "Do you think it has something to do with what happened with Judas and why he isn't here with us?" His only answer was some scattered shrugs.

"Why do you think he told me I would deny him?" Peter asked with a troubled expression. Then he mumbled to himself, "How could he ask such a question? The Master knows I would never desert him . . . doesn't he?"

Jesus heard them talking and was aware of their confusion and concern. As he neared his favorite place of prayer, he stopped, looked into their faces, and forced a smile. He so wanted to put his arms around them and explain it all in a way they could understand. But how could he? How could any human truly understand the spiritual war that was about to be waged between heaven and hell? Instead he said, "Pray that you will not fall into temptation."

He walked the twenty yards to his sacred spot and deeply inhaled the gentle wind. It was heavy with moisture. Spring growth fragranced the air with sweetness. How precious this piece of earth had become to him! He had spent countless hours here in communion with the Father. Here, the human and divine met in one body and spoke with one voice to achieve one outcome: the rescue and redemption of the world.

He paused, thinking about what the next twenty-four hours would bring. Then he opened his hands and looked at the palms

that had healed and comforted so many. He pressed a finger
hard into the center of his right hand and tried to imagine the
sensation of heavy spikes nailing his hands and feet to wood
beams. A shudder ran through his body. His humanity recoiled
against the pain he knew he must endure. When he closed his
eyes he could hear the venomous insults that would pierce his
heart. The angry voices left him cold and clammy. He opened
his eyes and turned them toward the night sky and thought of
home and Father. Overwhelmed with agony and loneliness, his
legs gave way. His knees hit the ground, and he fell forward at
the waist. The words spilled from his lips as if pouring from a
broken vessel. "Father, if you are willing, take this cup from me."
Then quietly . . . slowly, he added, "Yet not my will but yours be
done." Great tears of grief fell to the ground, and he hugged his
arms against his abdomen as he wept.

The angel Gabriel had been sent to the garden by the Father
to stand watch. The Father would send no other, for it was
Gabriel who had announced the coming of the Messiah to Mary,
and now he would be God's messenger of courage at the end of
Christ's life. He was sent to encourage and strengthen Jesus for
the brutal experience that would soon begin. Thus far, he had
watched and listened from the shadows. Now, he came and knelt
beside the suffering Savior. Gently engulfing Jesus with his powerful wings, Gabriel warmed his Lord against the chills that shiv-
ered through his body. Jesus lifted his head at the warm embrace
from heaven, and the eyes of heaven met the eyes of earth.

Locking his eyes on those of his Master, Gabriel said, "I have a message from the Father. These are his words: 'If I could remove you from this place and still save these people we love so deeply, you know I would. If I could wash away the sins of the world without your blood, I would not hesitate to end your agony. And even now, my son, you know that if you say the word the angel I have sent will call out and I will destroy all those who want to harm you. But I know you will not. Be strong and courageous, my Son. After you have suffered a little while, I will welcome you home."

Gabriel cradled Jesus in his arms. Being in anguish, Jesus prayed even more earnestly. His sweat fell like drops of blood to the ground. When he rose from prayer, Jesus knew the time had come. Gabriel put his strong hands on Jesus' shoulders, spread his wings wide, and placed his forehead against the Savior's. Looking into Jesus' eyes, Gabriel repeated three times, "The Father loves you; your blood will save the world."

When Jesus walked back to the disciples, he found them asleep. "Why are you sleeping?" he asked as he wakened them. "Get up and pray so that you will not fall into temptation."

Gabriel was filled with sadness as he watched the approaching crowd, led by Judas the betrayer, surround Jesus. As Judas leaned forward with a kiss of greeting for Jesus, Gabriel repeated to himself, "The Father loves you; your blood will save the world."

Scriptural Account

LUKE 22:39-46

Jesus went out as usual to the Mount of Olives, and his disciples followed him. On reaching the place, he said to them, "Pray that you will not fall into temptation." He withdrew about a stone's throw beyond them, knelt down and prayed, "Father, if you are willing, take this cup from me; yet not my will, but yours be done." An angel from heaven appeared to him and strengthened him. And being in anguish, he prayed more earnestly, and his sweat was like drops of blood falling to the ground.

When he rose from prayer and went back to the disciples, he found them asleep, exhausted from sorrow. "Why are you sleeping?" he asked them. "Get up and pray so that you will not fall into temptation."

17

A Messenger of Blessing

Introduction

If your life is basically trouble free, conflicts nonexistent, failures too few to mention, and disappointments seldom darken your door, you can skip right past this message. However, if you are like the rest of us, and it seems that every day presents some new dilemma, failures accumulate with age, and disappointments overshadow the starry-eyed dreams of youth, remember: *God blesses those who earnestly seek him.*

This promise glows like a beacon in our future and acts as a cleansing shower to our past. It plainly states that God blesses our simple faith. He does not measure your looks, accomplishments, wealth, or deeds before opening his arms and touching your life.

He doesn't tally your missteps, poor choices, or self-inflicted troubles before releasing his blessings. He wants only for you to want him, to pursue him—to step with a believing heart into his strong embrace. He will revive dead dreams and give birth to new visions.

Allow the hope of this promise to work into your wounds, cuts, and bruises like a soothing salve. Look at the kind of people who have already received this promise: The stumbling Peter walked on water and was the one honored to open the gates of heaven with the keys of the kingdom. A despised tax collector ate supper with a divine Savior and found salvation. Poor peasants were parents to the King of kings. Deserting disciples turned the world upside down. Two Mary's, armed with spices to cover the stench of death, were the first to find that failed hopes and dreams were alive. Good news? The best you will ever hear. You will never be disappointed while seeking God.

A Messenger of Blessing

Early Sunday morning, the sun crept slowly across the room, as if looking for someone to awaken. When it reached Mary's bed, it discovered her fully awake, her eyes swollen from hours of uncontrollable weeping. All night long, violent emotions had shaken her body and erupted in tears. Each eruption was followed by a series of trembling sighs as she tried to regain her composure. But the reprieve lasted only a few moments before she would be hit by another quake, and the whole process would begin again. Her entire body ached from the ordeal. The sunlight forced her awareness of the new day, and a sweet fragrance of freshly fallen rain graced her red nose. She took a deep breath, trying to ease her crying.

Mary Magdalene had never felt such agonizing sorrow. Not even her years of prostitution had produced the loneliness and heartache she now felt. All she had to do was whisper his name, and the whole scene—beating, insults, crucifixion—leaped freshly into her mind. Sleep had come in short snatches, and even then she dreamed of the crowd's relentless call for Christ's crucifixion. She had spent the Sabbath tearfully repeating unanswered questions: Why did they hate him so much? What did he ever do but love everyone he met—even a stained prostitute? She lifted her head and directed her questions heavenward: "O God, why did they kill my hope, my dreams, my life? I wish now I had died with him rather than face life without him." Her body heaved with the pain and tears sprang to her eyes once again.

Through her sobs she heard a voice: "Mary! Mary! Are you awake?" Recognizing the voice of her friend, Mary the mother of James, Mary Magdalene opened the door, and the two women fell into each other's arms. Muffling their wails so as not to disturb sleeping neighbors, the women comforted each other. Finally, Mary Magdalene pulled away and said, "Before we go to the tomb, let us pray the prayer Jesus taught us. Maybe it will ease our pain, if only for a few moments."

The two weeping women knelt together and prayed, "Our Father in Heaven, hallowed be your name." When Mary Magdalene's voice faltered, the other Mary continued alone, "Your kingdom come, your will be done, on earth as it is in heaven. . . ."

When they finished the Lord's Prayer, Mary the mother of James concluded, "And please let us know that everything will somehow be alright. Amen." Little did they know just how clearly their words were heard in heaven.

The angel Azael was poised and ready. Michael and Gabriel had been given the order to move the stone away from the tomb, and every heavenly being eagerly awaited word that Christ had risen. Joyful preparations had been made for the return of the Son to his place at the right hand of the Father. Summoned to the throne of the Most High, Azael approached the Father and knelt before him. "Almighty," he said, "your servant awaits your command."

"Azael, I have been touched by the prayers and petitions of two faithful servants who followed my Son to the Cross. They have chosen to visit the tomb this morning, but they will not understand what they will find there. Follow them to the grave, see that they are safe, and give them this message for me: 'He is not here; he has risen, just as he said.' Tell them they will see him again, and comfort them, for they are fretful and frightened."

As bidden, Azael flew to join the two Marys. The weeping women gathered the spices they had prepared for Jesus' body, shut the door to Mary Magdalene's home, and began the slow walk to the tomb where Jesus had been laid. Azael remained unseen so that he would not frighten the women. He watched as they walked hand in hand, clinging to each other for strength, singing songs of praise they had learned from Jesus. Tears streamed down their cheeks, and they stopped every so often to bolster each other's courage and ready themselves to face the sealed tomb, a symbol of their dead dreams. Azael felt a catch in his heart as he observed their pain. *Oh, how they loved their Lord,* he thought.

Along the way, Azael noticed angels of darkness everywhere. When they saw him, they hurled snarling taunts at him, but he said nothing in response. Instead, he moved closer to the women and spread his mighty wings around them to protect them from attack. Suddenly and without warning, the earth began to shake, and the horde of dark angels began to wail and scream. The women fell to their knees in terror, and Azael covered them to keep them safe. As Azael rose, he saw that all the angels of evil had fled. The women looked at each other, stunned, and asked simultaneously, "What was that?"

Shaken, they quickened their pace. As they approached the tomb, they saw that the stone had been rolled away. An angel of God sat upon it. The guards, thoroughly frightened, lay as still as dead men. The two Marys clung to each other in fear. Suddenly, Azael appeared to them. But he said, "Do not be afraid, for I know that you are looking for Jesus, who was crucified. He is not here; he has risen, just as he said." Azael's voice was calm and soothing, and his face glowed with joy; the women knew they had no reason to be afraid. He moved behind them and placed his strong arms around their shoulders and said, "Come and see the place where he lay. Then go quickly and tell his disciples: 'He has risen from the dead and is going ahead of you into Galilee. There you will see him.' Now I have told you."

Amazed, the women hurried away as Azael had directed. Just a few yards from the tomb, the Savior appeared to them. "Greetings," Jesus said. Both women fell to the ground, grabbed hold of his feet, and worshiped him. Azael knelt directly behind them. Jesus said to the women, "Do not be afraid. Go and tell my brothers to go to Galilee; there they will see me."

As the women, now full of joy, danced toward the city, Jesus smiled approvingly at Azeal and sighed, "Oh, how I love my people." And Azael answered, "And how they love you, my Lord."

Scriptural Account

MATTHEW 28:1-10 (SEE ALSO LUKE 24:1-10)

After the Sabbath, at dawn on the first day of week, Mary Magdalene and the other Mary went to look at the tomb.

There was a violent earthquake, for an angel of the Lord came down from heaven and, going to the tomb, rolled back the stone and sat on it. His appearance was like lightning, and his clothes were white as snow. The guards were so afraid of him that they shook and became like dead men.

The angel said to the women, "Do not be afraid, for I know that you are looking for Jesus, who was crucified. He is not here; he has risen, just as he said. Come and see the place where he lay. Then go quickly and tell his disciples: 'He has risen from the dead and is going ahead of you into Galilee. There you will see him.' Now I have told you."

So the women hurried away from the tomb, afraid yet filled with joy, and ran to tell his disciples. Suddenly Jesus met them. "Greetings," he said. They came to him, clasped his feet and worshiped him. Then Jesus said to them, "Do not be afraid. Go and tell my brothers to go to Galilee; there they will see me."

18

MESSENGERS OF HOPE

Introduction

Have you noticed that most people avoid saying "Good-bye"? Usually they prefer "see you later" or "see ya" or just "later." Good-byes are hard to say and even harder to hear. Who doesn't remember a poignant tearful farewell to cherished colleagues, treasured friends, precious parents, or valued neighbors? We don't enjoy the pain of final good-byes.

We like a little hope attached to our departures; we like to believe that we will see that special someone again. There is permanence to the word good-bye that we would rather not think about—but there doesn't have to be. Even though we know that someday, sometime, somewhere we will have to say good-bye to someone, it doesn't have to be forever. There is One who has challenged the everlasting nature of good-bye. He appeared on the other side of death and said, "I will come back for you." He even sent angelic messengers of hope to affirm the sacred covenant. He broke the restraint of the grave that enslaves humankind to this world and said, "You will be with me where I am."

Jesus' extraordinary promise of return has caused a thunderous echo of hope to ring in countless hearts for more than two thousand years: Hope for families who have been separated by too much distance and too few resources. Hope for friendships that were set for a life-time when one of the lives ended abruptly. Hope for parents who had to say unexpected good-byes to children taken by a destructive disease or a tragic accident. Hope for husbands and wives whose lifelong partner's physical hearts stopped while their spiritual love continued to beat strong.

As you experience the uncertainty of everyday existence, don't forget to keep an eye on the heavens. That's where he will appear. His resurrection marked the end to final farewells, his return will mark the end of good-byes forever, and his gathering of God's children will give birth to an eternal chorus of hellos.

Messengers of Hope

The morning was rich with sunlight and summer heat as the apostles gathered on the eastern slope of the Mount of Olives. It had been forty days since Christ had come out of the tomb and shown himself to the disciples. Gone from the apostles' thoughts were the bitter images of the crucifixion—the murderous insults hurled by the spitting crowds, the severe beating that staggered the Savior's steady march to the cross, the crown of thorns that mocked his royalty. These could find no suitable housing in the hearts and minds of the disciples who were filled with joy in the presence of their Lord.

Peter's denial of Christ had been transformed from a flaming fire of guilt into a glowing ember by Christ's tender confrontation. Peter felt restored in every way. Though Satan would use the denial to accuse Peter in the future, Christ's love would extinguish the fear and doubt. The desertion of the chosen ones at the arrest scene in the garden, and Thomas' post-resurrection disbelief, had become distant memories. Christ had embraced each one at some point in his precious time with them and told them they were forgiven. There was no room for the heavy weight of guilt in the future Christ had planned for them. The apostles would need to be focused and free of encumbrances in order to accomplish their mission to share the Good News of Christ with the world.

Each day the apostles had spent with Christ since the resurrection overflowed with building hope and swelling courage. However, in a sad and serious way, these last few days had been different from all the other days they had spent with the Savior. Final words had been spoken. Warnings had been issued. Jesus' instructions had been explicit and exact. Just yesterday, as the eleven met with him, he had stood before each one, placed his hands on their shoulders, looked into their faces, and spoken from his heart: "Peter, stay strong in your convictions and never look back. Pain will accompany you in this life, but peace will ultimately reign." With tears in his eyes he had said, "John, my beloved, our friendship is a treasure for your heart. I will eagerly await our reunion." He had continued down the line of tear-stained faces until he had spoken a special blessing on each one.

The dreaded good-bye hung in the air, but none of them wanted to hear it, especially not from the mouth of the One they had hoped would stay forever. So when they met together, John asked him, "Lord, are you going to restore the kingdom to Israel at this time?" The question was laced with hope. They all hungered for him to answer, "Yes, I am going to stay and rule here on earth," or "Yes, and you will be by my side." But those were not his words. They all sensed that the dreaded farewell was imminent.

He said to them, "It is not for you to know the times or dates the Father has set by his own authority. But you will receive power when the Holy Spirit comes on you; and you will be my witnesses in Jerusalem, and in all Judea and Samaria, and to the ends of the earth."

Then he was taken up before their eyes, and a cloud hid him from their sight. With hands shielding their weeping eyes from the sun, they watched, hoping he would appear one last time.

As they looked intently into the sky, two men dressed in white suddenly stood beside them. One was the angel Oriel, and the other, Stalel. The Father had chosen these particular celestials to be present at this sad scene because of their gifts of encouragement and comfort. He had given them a message of hope for the chosen followers that would take the sting from this painful parting.

Stalel placed his arms around the shoulders of Philip and Thomas; Oriel held the arms of Peter and James. They looked toward heaven with them for a moment, then with broad smiles and warm voices they said, "Men of Galilee, why do you stand here looking at the sky? This same Jesus, who has been taken from you into heaven, will come back in the same way you have seen him go."

The words hit their targets. The hearts of the apostles filled with hope. The tears soon dried and their feet barely touched the ground as they made their way back to town.

The apostles would speak often about the last day they spent with the Lord of lords. And wherever they shared the news of the ascension, they encouraged the faith of the saints with the message of God delivered by angels: *Jesus will come back in the same way we saw him go into heaven.* And the message always hit home.

Scriptural Account

ACT 1:1-11

In my former book, Theophilus, I wrote about all that Jesus began to do and to teach until the day he was taken up to heaven, after giving instructions through the Holy Spirit to the apostles he had chosen. After his suffering, he showed himself to these men and gave many convincing proofs that he was alive. He appeared to them over a period of forty days and spoke about the kingdom of God. On one occasion, while he was eating with them, he gave them this command: "Do not leave Jerusalem, but wait for the gift my Father promised, which you have heard me speak about. For John baptized with water, but in a few days you will be baptized with the Holy Spirit."

So when they met together, they asked him, "Lord, are you at this time going to restore the kingdom to Israel?"

He said to them: "It is not for you to know the times or dates the Father has set by his own authority. But you will receive power when the Holy Spirit comes on you; and you will be my witnesses in Jerusalem, and in all Judea and Samaria, and to the ends of the earth."

After he said this, he was taken up before their very eyes, and a cloud hid him from their sight.

They were looking intently up into the sky as he was going, when suddenly two men dressed in white stood beside them. "Men of Galilee," they said, "why do you stand here looking into the sky?

This same Jesus, who has been taken from you into heaven, will come back in the same way you have seen him go into heaven."

19

A Messenger of Freedom

Introduction

Keys are amazing things, aren't they? Already today, you have probably used keys to open a door, start a car, or lock something of value away. What pocket or purse doesn't jingle with the familiar sound of metal keys colliding in rhythm to each step? Who hasn't felt the panic of realizing that keys have been misplaced? Without keys, much of what we value would remain on the other side of a locked door—so near, yet out of reach forever.

You possess one particular key that performs the unexplainable, the unimaginable, even the miraculous. It unlocks prison doors, opens closed hearts, frees frozen relationships, and protects priceless souls. It is not fashioned from metal, plastic, aluminum, or wood; rather its power is rooted in eternity, and it is activated by your faith. That key is prayer.

Use it, and use it often. It won't wear out; in fact, it becomes stronger each time you insert it into a lock. Use it to escape the prison cell of worry or fear. Turn it to release imprisoned love for God and others. Unlock relationships that have become cold and constricted. Release the protective power of the Almighty God.

Pray, and watch the shackles of sin fall away. Pray, and find fear replaced by peace. Pray, and discover union with the Creator of all. Lift your heart in times of celebration and release thankful joy. Enter the throne room of the Heavenly Father and find the door to his heart standing wide open. Come by yourself or with family and friends. Don't let the dust of neglect collect on your key to freedom.

The world may attempt to imprison you with pain and confusion, but you need not be bound. Open your heart, lift your head, and turn the key.

A Messenger of Freedom

The gloom of the moonless night reflected the hearts and spirits of the people of Jerusalem, especially Jesus' disciples. The events of the previous days orchestrated by an increasingly bloodthirsty King Herod, had produced a raw tension in the church. The horrific sound of the blade cutting through the neck of James, beloved brother of John, still echoed in the ears of saints across the city. The morbid pleasure this execution brought to many Jews incited Herod to pursue and punish Peter.

Every believer who had witnessed Peter's arrest at the temple spent the afternoon spreading the chilling details about the heavily armed soldiers who harshly escorted Peter to prison. They also told of Peter's instructions to those around him while being led away, "Whatever happens, fear not; God is with us."

In homes throughout Jerusalem, believers gathered to mount a prayer vigil. They petitioned the Father to act quickly to free the apostle who had helped so many others find freedom in Christ. Some prayed boldly in thundering voices, others trembled with timidity, but all were urgent in their pleas, begging God to intercede.

Heaven heard. A call went out to the angel Aphesel. As always, when an urgent need for deliverance from danger arose, Aphesel was the first to be summoned. His superb strength could break a thousand chains, and no angel could move undetected through the forces of evil as well as he. He had shut the mouths of lions when Daniel was thrown in their den, and he was there when Gideon had led the three hundred against the threat of the Midianites. His radiance was breathtaking, his sparkling eyes intense and alert, his heart loyal to the Father. He hated the schemes and conspiracies of Satan with every fiber of his being.

The archangel Michael found Aphesel at the gates of the throne room. "Aphesel," Michael said, "the prayers of thousands of God's children have reached the Father. He is aware of their heartache and wants them to know that he loves them and is attentive to their requests. Go quickly; Peter is in prison. He has accepted his imminent death, and he is not afraid. Release him and deliver him from the plans of the evil one so that God's children will be assured in their faith. But move carefully, Satan wishes to destroy Peter. He believes that by doing so, he can defeat the church here and now. We must remind him that nothing will defeat what the Father has begun in his beloved children."

Swiftly and unseen, Aphesel made his way to Israel. As he passed Herod's palace, he was stunned by the number of angels of darkness he saw there. They guarded the doors and perimeter of the palace against any effort by the Father to rescue Herod from his hardened heart. Aphesel thought to himself, *If the Almighty would give the order, I would speed past you and into the presence of Herod before you could recite one more of your deceptions.* But that was not his mission today.

Aphesel reached the prison that held Peter and moved quickly into his cell. He smiled in amusement when he saw how the soldiers had attempted to insure Peter's captivity—by binding him with chains and surrounding him with soldiers, even as he slept. "You will have to do better than that to keep a child of God in prison," he said as he moved toward the sleeping figures. Amazed by how soundly Peter slept, Aphesel thought to himself, *Only a disciple of the Lord could sleep like this in prison while facing death.* He then struck Peter on the side to wake him. "Quick, get up!" he said, and the chains instantly fell from Peter's wrists. Then Aphesel said to him, "Put on your clothes and sandals. Wrap your cloak around you and follow me."

Peter followed Aphesel out of the prison but had no idea that what was happening was real; he thought he was seeing a vision. They passed the first and second guards and came to the iron gate leading into the city. The heavy gate creaked and groaned as Aphesel powered it open. They walked through together and remained silent for the length of one street. Then, sure that he had accomplished his mission. Aphesel suddenly left.

Peter came to himself and said, "Now I know without a doubt that the Lord sent his angel and rescued me from Herod's clutches and from everything the Jewish people were anticipating."

Peter hurried to the house of Mary the mother of John, where many people had gathered to pray. When Peter knocked at the outer entrance, a servant girl, who had been praying earnestly with the rest of the gathered disciples, came to the door. She recognized Peter's voice and was so excited that she ran back without opening the door. "Peter is at the door!" she exclaimed. But no one would believe her. When they finally opened the door and saw him, they were astonished.

Peter motioned them to be quiet, and he described how the Lord had sent an angel to bring him out of prison. "The Lord heard your prayer for my deliverance, and he has provided. He has once more revealed that he loves us and is attentive to our prayers. Tell James and the brothers all that has happened." In leaving, he said, "Remember my words: whatever happens, fear not; God is with us."

Back in heaven, when Aphesel reported the rescue of Peter, Michael embraced him and said, "Well done, faithful Aphesel." Aphesel then returned to his post and awaited his next call from the Father to rescue a suffering saint or deliver a child from danger.

Scriptural Account

ACTS 12:1-17

It was about this time that King Herod arrested some who belonged to the church, intending to persecute them. He had James, the brother of John, put to death with the sword. When he saw that this pleased the Jews, he proceeded to seize Peter also. This happened during the Feast of Unleavened Bread. After arresting him, he put him in prison, handing him over to be guarded by four squads of four soldiers each. Herod intended to bring him out for public trial after the Passover.

So Peter was kept in prison, but the church was earnestly praying to God for him.

The night before Herod was to bring him to trial, Peter was sleeping between two soldiers, bound with two chains, and sentries stood guard at the entrance. Suddenly an angel of the Lord appeared and a light shone in the cell. He struck Peter on the side and woke him up. "Quick, get up!" he said, and the chains fell off Peter's wrists.

Then the angel said to him, "Put on your clothes and sandals." And Peter did so. "Wrap your cloak around you and follow me," the angel told him. Peter followed him out of the prison, but he had no idea that what the angel was doing was really happening; he thought he was seeing a vision. They passed the first and second guards and came to the iron gate leading to the city. It opened for them by itself, and they went through it. When they had walked the length of one street, suddenly the angel left him.

Then Peter came to himself and said, "Now I know without a doubt that the Lord sent his angel and rescued me from Herod's clutches and from everything the Jewish people were anticipating."

When this had dawned on him, he went to the house of Mary the mother of John, also called Mark, where many people had gathered and were praying. Peter knocked at the outer entrance, and a servant girl named Rhoda came to answer the door. When she recognized Peter's voice, she was so overjoyed she ran back without opening it and exclaimed, "Peter is at the door!"

"You're out of your mind," they told her. When she kept insisting that it was so, they said, "It must be his angel."

But Peter kept on knocking, and when they had opened the door and saw him, they were astonished. Peter motioned with his hand for them to be quiet and described how the Lord had brought him out of prison. "Tell James and the brothers about this," he said, and then he left for another place.

SECTION SIX

GIVE

20

FOREVER FRIENDS

Introduction

Get ready for a very nice compliment you will most certainly want to hear. It may come as a shock to you, but to those who know you best, it is an accepted fact. No, it's not about your youthful good looks or irresistible charm. It is something even better, and it fits you just right. The compliment is that you are a good friend who is always there and you have some very good friends who love you and need you.

Oh, you probably don't think about it much, but others do—for you bring caring, comfort, courage, and assurance into the lives of your friends.

Isn't that the true blessing of friendship? When the cold wind of doubt sweeps through a heart, it is a friend like you who brings a warm embrace that ignites within the soul a fire of cozy confidence. If the future of a friend begins to look bleak, there you are cheering her on with encouraging words and unrelenting faith. You shed fresh tears with those who hurt, celebrate with those who receive good news, pick up those who fall down, and quietly listen to those who are aching to be heard.

Yes, that's you at the birthday party serving others and saving the day. You are the emergency baby-sitter, the one to pick up the last-minute item from the store, and the one who friends call first when they need someone to talk to. You are there at giddy graduations, ghastly recitals, and grim grave sites. Quite simply, you are like one who greeted friends at an empty tomb with the words "Do not be afraid," and gave them the assurance that friendship is forever.

Forever Friends

As the first light of day crept across the room, it discovered two figures kneeling on the floor, side by side, arms draped across each other's shoulders, praying. When one woman would falter and begin to weep, the other would take up the prayer until she could no longer go on.

Over the last couple of years, these two women had shared more than most friends share in a lifetime. They had shared aspirations and dreams, causes and concerns, fights and failures. They had walked the same paths, eaten the same meals, slept under the same stars, and above all, followed the same man—a man they believed in; a man they had seen heal the lame, blind, and broken, and even raise the dead—a man they had watched suffer and die just the past Friday evening. Now, on Sunday morning they shared their common grief.

They were two of the most unlikely friends in the world. Everyone who knew them commented on the irony of their shared name, because their similarities stopped there. Mary the mother of James was short, stout, silver-haired, and soft-spoken. Her kind eyes, fixed smile, and sweet disposition made her a beacon of light to friends and strangers alike. If neighbors, friends, or family experienced joy or tragedy, success or failure, hopefulness or heartbreak, Mary was the first to know. She was the consummate encourager and could always be trusted with confidence or confession.

Mary Magdalene, on the other hand had once been possessed by seven demons. Jesus had driven them out of her and Mary had followed him ever since. She was tall and slim, with coal black hair that hung all the way down past her waist. Her features were chiseled and sharp. Although her expression had softened some since her liberation, a stubborn harness remained. Mary possessed an inexhaustible enthusiasm and outspokenness that some found threatening but the other Mary found wonderfully refreshing.

They had become immediate friends when, after the exorcism, Jesus arranged for the other Mary to come and minister to her. Mary Magdalene talked for hours to the other Mary about the horrors of the possession and how it had affected her. The other Mary had listened unwaveringly and watched intently as tears washed away years of pain and suffering. From that night on, they were the best of friends, growing in their faith and devoting themselves to helping others.

But their faith was not strong now. They spoke with uncertainty, prayed in desperation, and wondered what would happen since the center of their lives had been murdered.

After watching Joseph of Arimathea close the grave of Jesus on Friday evening by rolling a large stone in front of the tomb, they had committed to come back together on Sunday. They felt that just being near the body of Jesus might soothe the immense pain they felt at the loss of the One they loved so very much. So on this early Sunday morning, they rose from their prayers, gathered the spices they hoped to place on Jesus body, closed the door to Mary Magdalene's house, and hesitantly started for the grave site.

The two Marys walked hand in hand and inhaled deeply the fresh sweetness left in the air by an early morning rain-fall. They attempted to sing some of the songs of worship that Jesus had taught them, but with every familiar verse, they pictured Jesus moving his arms to the beat of the song, encouraging the disciples to pick up the tune, and they would dissolve into tears.

The two women had to stop several times and bolster each other's courage to face the sealed tomb. They thought their dreams lay dead in that tomb. They believed their journey had ended. They wondered what they would do now. Little did they know that their friendship, faith, and future were about to be reignited, lit by the friend they thought they had lost.

With the tomb not one hundred yards away, the earth suddenly began to shake violently. It knocked both Marys to the ground. They held each other tightly until the tremors ceased. They held each other tightly until the tremors ceased. They looked at each other and asked simultaneously, "What was that?"

Trembling and shaken, they began walking quickly toward the tomb. When they arrived, they were startled by the scene before them. The stone had been rolled away, and an angel of God sat upon it. The guards who had been watching the tomb lay as motionless as dead men. Both

Marys gasped, covered their mouths with their hands, and dropped the spices they were carrying.

The angel said to the women, "Do not be afraid, for I know that you are looking for Jesus, who was crucified. He is not here; He has risen, just as He said." He moved behind them and placed his arms around their shoulders. "Come and see the place where He lay. Then go quickly and tell His disciples: 'He has risen from and is going ahead of you into Galilee. There you will see Him.' Now I have told you."

When the women finally realized it was true—that their beloved Jesus was not dead but alive—they embraced each other and began to weep with joy. They then turned, arm in arm, and hurried away from the tomb and toward Galilee.

Suddenly, just a few yards from the tomb, Jesus stood before them. Smiling warmly, he said, "Greetings." The two Marys came to him, clasped his feet, and worshiped him. Then Jesus said to them, "Do not be afraid. Go and tell my brothers to go to Galilee; there they will see me."

As the two women, now full of joy, skipped and danced toward the city, they sang their favorite song Jesus had taught them. Their friendship had tasted the bitterness of loss and the sweetness of resurrection. They were assured in their hearts that their friendship would last a lifetime, and now, well beyond.

Scriptural Account
MATTHEW 28:1-10

After the Sabbath, at dawn on the first day of the week, Mary Magdalene and the other Mary went to look at the tomb.

There was a violent earthquake, for an angel of the Lord came down from heaven and, going to the tomb, rolled back the stone and sat on it. His appearance was like lightning, and his clothes were white as snow. The guards were so afraid to him that they shook and became like dead men.

The angel said to the women, "Do not be afraid, for I know that you are looking for Jesus, who was crucified. He is not here; he has risen, just as he said. Come and see the place where he lay. Then go quickly and tell his disciples: 'He has risen from the dead and is going ahead of you into Galilee. There you will see him.' Now I have told you."

So the women hurried away from the tomb, afraid yet filled with joy, and ran to tell his disciples. Suddenly Jesus met them. "Greetings," he said. They came to him, clasped his feet and worshiped him. Then Jesus said to them, "Do not be afraid. Go and tell my brothers to go to Galilee; there they will see me."

21

MET BY MERCY

Introduction

Here is a question that may take some ardent meditation, though for some it may come quickly. When I began pondering the question myself I had to admit, the answer surprised me, or should I say answers. Are you ready for the question? Have you ever experienced being thoroughly soaked in mercy? Take your time, maybe even a day or two, and scour through your memories, because if you discover about yourself, what I discovered about myself, it will be a life changer.

I want you to fully understand what I mean by *mercy*, without question or assumption. I am not talking about a touch or even a hearty portion of mercy. Have you ever been in a soul-saturating, heart-washing, thirst-quenching rainfall of mercy granted to you from either earth or heaven? Perhaps it came from a hurtful stab of words you inflicted on a friend which threatened to deaden feelings cherished for years. But then the friend chose to bury the weapon you used, and said, "Forget it. I have." And that friend was true to their word. That is being soaked in mercy.

Such mercy may have come in the form of a spouse who turned more than a cheek—who remained faithful through a soul-slapping affair which ended with your forgiveness, and a complete covering of scars. You are loved even now, as though it never happened; you have never heard a word mentioned. That is being soaked in mercy.

It may be that you remember standing at a cross more than once, watching a figure covered in wounds speak your name as he pushed against the nails, for one last gasp, to ask the Father for your forgiveness. And you suddenly realized that it was you who had the hammer in your hand. Now that's being soaked in mercy.

Why is it important to remember these experiences when they bring such pain? First of all, as you recall those heavy drops of mercy, you might recognize that they were bitter ends to a much desired and sweeter beginning. The pains of childbirth always precede the miracle of new life. You will also be able to see that your heart was changed by such events—that they shaped the person you are now. But most of all you will sense what a rich gift mercy is, and you in turn will be able to drench others in that same life changing mercy.

Pain surrounds us at every turn. A great deal of it is self inflicted and it is burying generations in a wasteland of sandy foundations. You see it on the frowning faces of those you work with, and hear it in the sharp tones of bitter tongues, covered in guilt. You met or spoke with someone today who is cornered by failures and can't see a way out. You are a constant lifestream of mercy with the ability to quench the drought of this world: speak mercy, show mercy, and above all point to mercy with your words and with your life. It is there at the cross, and it is an abundant rainfall that is ready to soak all who come. You remember don't you? You yourself are soaked to the skin in it. You remember how wonderful those drops of life giving moisture felt to your arid heart. Go pour that out on someone you know or meet today. And whatever you do leave your umbrella at home.

Met by Mercy

Leah's rich brown eyes were ablaze in fear as she was violently dragged down the narrow street that led from her home. Her left wrist burned and grew white in the grip of a man she had never seen or met before. She knew he was a Pharisee by his heavy religious adornment that made noise with every step. He was completely silent except for heavy breathing as he marched resolutely toward a destination that was clear only to him. Leah was keenly aware of a great crowd of men that followed close behind, and she could hear their bitter verbal assaults. She could feel their trails of spit land on her shoulders. She could also sense their lustful stares at her half naked body. Leah clutched the sheet she had attempted to cover herself with when three men burst into her modest home and yanked her from the bed she shared with Samuel.

She heard herself say his name and ask, "Samuel, where is Samuel?" She wondered if he was safe. One thing was for sure—he wasn't with her. For two years now he had come to her home every week and spent the night making promises of love and commitment which he would fulfill as soon as he disposed of his wife. She had fallen for the sugar-laced lines because, after her previous husband had divorced her, she was desperate for love and security.

His handsome youth, dark, wavy hair and strong body, combined with his gentle ways, were irresistible. He was a perfect match for a thirty-year-old woman whose beauty was hard to miss. Leah was tall and slender and full of life, with dark smooth skin, rich, brown hair, and a bashful smile that truly gleamed. Samuel had often asked her why in the world her former husband had divorced her. She never told him the truth about the woman her husband had left her for. It was an indictment she refused to let land on her.

She hoped Samuel was somewhere near and would somehow come to speak up for her and free her from this growing mob that now filled the street from every side. As the voices grew louder behind her she knew she was in serious trouble. For the first time she dropped all the defensive thoughts and excuses and realized she was an adulteress, and she knew what that meant. There really was no defense.

Under the weight of the thought she stumbled and fell and the sheet came off, exposing her to everyone. Someone reached out and draped the sheet back over her but was aggressively pushed away by the man she didn't know. He reached down and almost pulled her arm out of its socket before she regained her footing. Her bare legs and feet, dragging along the harsh surface of the street, were now marked with deep gashes and bloody streams. As she attempted to look back at the person that helped her she noticed that everyone in the crowd held stones in their hands. Where did they find all of these jagged stones? They weren't lying in the streets within the city walls. They must have been planning on this morning's event and brought them from outside the city. It dawned on her that her life was about to be over and someone had laid the trap. She asked herself again: *Where is Samuel?*

As they rounded the corner the noise of the crowd was deafening. She now understood their destination. They were going to the temple courts. But why? If they were going to kill her why didn't they just take her outside the city gates and do the deed? A nervous sweat now began to drench her body under the sheet. Her hair lay across her face in damp strands, and the dread in her eyes was now tempered by surrender. The end was near and her shameful demise would happen in the courts of the temple of her God. She was suddenly reminded of the years she had spent in faithful service to her God before she met Samuel. Where had her faith escaped to? Now an even greater horror assaulted her—the dreadful fear of a holy God. What had she done?

Entering the temple courts there was no hesitation on the part of the man who pulled on her or the crowd that followed. They headed straight for another crowd, not quite as large, gathered around a man sitting on a step and teaching. Leah noticed that he was not adorned with any of the religious garb her captor wore. He wore a simple cloak, and he smiled as he spoke. She wondered for a split second if the hard breathing Pharisee that now pushed her toward this plain man had ever smiled in his life.

Leah stood trembling, cold, and exposed. She looked down and saw her bloody feet and legs and felt streams running down her cheeks. Tears of fear, shame, and heartbreaking regret now spilled on the ground in front of this new man she had never seen or met before. She whispered softly to herself, "What now?"

The Pharisee ran his hands down his chest length beard, stood proudly before Jesus and the silenced crowds, and stated in defiance, "Teacher, this woman was caught in the act of adultery. In the Law Moses commanded us to stone such women. Now what do you say?" The Pharisee then took a step back and continued to brush his hands down his salt and pepper beard. They were using this question as a trap, in order to have a basis for accusing him.

But Jesus bent down and started to write on the ground with his finger. Leah watched him intently but could not see what he was writing. When they kept on questioning him, he straightened up and said to them, "If any of you is without sin, let him be the first to throw a stone at her." Again, he stooped down and wrote on the ground. Leah prepared herself to feel the first of the heavy stones rip against her flesh.

At this, those who heard began to go away one at a time, the older ones first, until only Jesus was left, with the woman still standing there. Jesus straightened up and asked her, "Woman, where are they? Has no one condemned you?"

Leah looked around her and saw they had all left. "No one, sir," she said.

"Then neither do I condemn you," Jesus declared, "Go now and leave your life of sin."

Jesus gave her an assuring smile and sat back down to teach. Stunned by her freedom, she stood for a few minutes and allowed the words to find a home in her heart. "I'm still alive, I'm still alive." She whispered to herself over and over again. As she turned to leave she looked down at what Jesus had written: *I desire mercy not sacrifice* were the words in the dirt. She could hear him as he resumed his teaching saying, "I am the light of the world. Whoever follows me will never walk in darkness, but will have the light of life." She pondered this as she left the temple courts that should have been her tomb.

Leah walked quickly to her home, cleaned her wounds, and wrote a note for Samuel she had delivered to him before running back to find Jesus. The note read, "I have been granted mercy and I in turn give mercy to you. Never come back to my home again. I hope you find the love of God as I have." She became a faithful follower of Jesus . . . all the way to the cross.

Scriptural Account
JOHN 8: 1-12

*But Jesus went to the Mount of Olives. At dawn he appeared
again in the temple courts, where all the people gathered around
him, and he sat down to teach them. The teachers of the law and
the Pharisees brought in a woman caught in adultery. They made
her stand before the group and said to Jesus, "Teacher, this woman
was caught in the act of adultery. In the Law Moses commanded
us to stone such women. Now what do you say?" They were using
this question as a trap, in order to have a basis for accusing him.*

*But Jesus bent down and started to write on the ground with
his finger. When they kept on questioning him, he straightened up
and said to them, "If any one of you is without sin, let him be the
first to throw a stone at her." Again, he stooped down and wrote
on the ground.*

*At this, those who heard began to go away one at a time, the
older ones first, until only Jesus was left, with the woman still
standing there. Jesus straightened up and asked her, "Woman,
where are they? Has no one condemned you?"*

"No one, sir," she said.

*"Then neither do I condemn you," Jesus declared. "Go now and
leave your life of sin."*

*When Jesus spoke again to the people, he said, "I am the light
of the world. Whoever follows me will never walk in darkness, but
will have the light of life."*